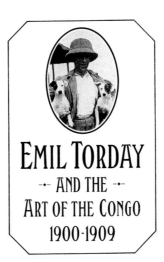

EMIL TORDAY
·+· AND THE ·+·
ART OF THE CONGO
1900·1909

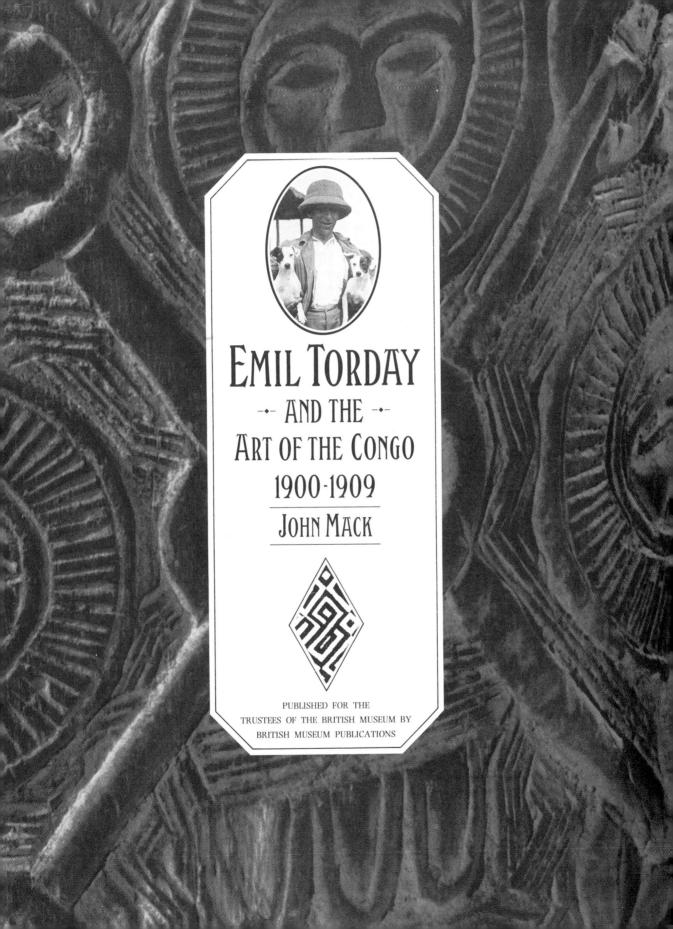

EMIL TORDAY

-·- AND THE -·-

ART OF THE CONGO

1900·1909

JOHN MACK

PUBLISHED FOR THE
TRUSTEES OF THE BRITISH MUSEUM BY
BRITISH MUSEUM PUBLICATIONS

© The Trustees of the British Museum

Published by British Museum Publications Ltd
46 Bloomsbury Street, London WC1B 3QQ

British Library Cataloguing in Publication Data
Mack, John
    Emil Torday and the art of the Congo, 1900–1909.
    1. Congolese visual arts, history
    I. Title   II. British Museum, *Trustees*
    709.6724

    ISBN 0-7141-1594-0

Designed by Harry Green

Set in Monophoto Photina
and printed in Great Britain by
BAS Printers Limited, Over Wallop, Hampshire

Pages 2–3 Detail of an old drum illustrated on p. 74.
Cover Wood 'portrait' figure representing Shyaam aMbul aNgoong, the founder of the Kuba kingdom. He ruled in the first half of the 17th century, though the figure was probably carved in the late 18th century. Kuba-Bushoong. 1909.12–10.1. H. 54.5 cm.
Inset Torday and his dogs, Duke and Sanga.
Background Detail of raffia textile illustrated on p. 18.

Contents

Preface

This book is one of two to be published by British Museum Publications which derive from the life and work of the Hungarian ethnographer Emil Torday (1875–1931). In the opening decades of the century Torday established a special relationship with the British Museum, although he was never formally employed as a member of its staff. The large and important collection of Central African art and artefacts which he formed for this institution remains the most important single collection in its holdings from that part of Africa, and arguably one of the richest and best documented early collections from anywhere on the continent. It contains some of the most frequently illustrated and familiar examples of the art of Africa. The second publication, a complete catalogue of the Torday collection (some 3,000 objects), is also in preparation (Mack forthcoming).

In one aspect this volume can be read as an introduction to that larger work. Its most immediate intent, however, is to supplement and expand on some of the themes raised in an exhibition of the Torday collection, which is held by the British Museum's Department of Ethnography at the Museum of Mankind. One of the aims of the exhibition is to survey the remarkable arts of the southern Congo State (now Zaire) as they were in the opening decade of the century. For a period of nine years from 1900 Torday travelled extensively, and virtually without interruption, through the region. That it should be possible to contemplate a major exhibition of this kind by drawing on the work of a single person is already an indication of Torday's achievement.

Torday – a distinguished African explorer in his own right – was also involved in a broader intellectual adventure. At the time the study of African culture, other than as a sideline to travel and exploration, was only beginning to get off the ground. Limiting conceptions of the cultures of the 'Dark Continent' still prevailed. In France particularly the art of some parts of Africa began to be appreciated, and, indeed, appropriated to European tastes. But the idea that such art might represent a more basic, raw strain of human expression remained important. From one point of view this kind of interest, however creative an inspiration for European artists, represented little advance for the image of Africa over the tenets of nineteenth-century social evolutionary thinking. For that perception to change significantly a different view of the integrity of African culture was needed. The ethnographic approach to African forms of expression, of which Torday was one of the pioneers, was thus a significant moment.

In Britain, as elsewhere, the subject of anthropology was still being formulated as a university discipline, and was yet to become established as a viable profession. As the new century dawned, it existed more or less as the province of museums and learned societies. Much of the impetus that was to lead to its establishment in universities in the present century came from studies of Oceanic peoples. In an African context Torday, though he remained entirely independent of educational and institutional employment, was a leading figure and exemplar. He was not in the first instance a scientist, but he was a sympathetic participant in the life of the peoples amongst whom he travelled as an administrative official, a trader, and latterly as the leader of an expedition. Not the least of his gifts was as a linguist. He was in at the birth of documentary fieldwork in Africa.

This book, then, is not a conventional exhibition catalogue: it is at once a discussion of the significance of the objects displayed, an essay in intellectual history, and an introduction to the art and anthropology of a part of Central Africa. That it should be so is perhaps because it is also, partly, a biographical account of an engaging, and at times a maverick, subject.

The prospect of undertaking a review of the Torday collection has been a preoccupation for the past twelve or so years during which I have also been involved in other curatorial concerns, and in undertaking my own fieldwork elsewhere in Africa. In that time I have benefited from discussions and correspondence with a number of other colleagues with Central African interests. Margret Carey, Mme van Geluwe, Albert Maesen and Jan Vansina have all been kind enough to respond to my general queries. In preparing the exhibition and this book I have been grateful for the encouragement and comments of Nigel Barley, David Binkley, Celia Clear, Annie Coombes, Pat Darish, Dunja Hersak, Malcolm McLeod, Rosalind Poignant and Enid Schilkrout. As on several previous occasions, I have benefited from a sympathetic editor in Deborah Wakeling. Janet Wallace and Christopher Date have helped to locate material in the British Museum Archives, as have the staff of the Department of Ethnography Library. Janos Kubassek's powers of perseverance in hunting down information about his fellow-countryman and sharing his observations have been of assistance. Finally, the exhibition has impinged upon the time and patience of many, but principally that of Bob Eckett, Julie Hudson and Christopher Spring, who have all responded with unstinting enthusiasm.

Difficulty has been occasioned by trying to match up Torday's use of terms and place-names with contemporary usage. For present purposes accepted modern renderings have as far as possible been adopted. As for the Kuba, Torday often used Luba terminology rather than local spelling. This has been rectified as appropriate. The term Congo or Congo State has been retained only because it refers to a specific historical entity, and the discussion that follows all concerns the pre-Independence period of modern Zaire.

All the illustrations here derive directly from the Torday expeditions. The objects are all from the Torday collections, the field photographs from his photographic archives, and the paintings were all commissioned by him from Norman Hardy. Mrs M. McElwain prepared the maps.

I   *Patterns in the darkness*

Joseph Conrad's *Heart of Darkness* was published in 1902. The 'darkness' of the title is at one level an inner moral state. Mistah Kurtz, the subject of the book dies at the precise moment he plumbs the depths of his own being and finds there only horror and despair. By extension his spiritual turmoil has been seen as standing for the condition of that whole generation which saw in the new century. Kurtz's journey into the soul, however, is also a journey in space, and the darkness a condition metaphorically associated with the place these events unfold, a river leading deep into a primal jungle – the Congo, which Conrad himself had visited as a seaman – the dark heart of the Dark Continent.

By 1902 the Congo was also experiencing another kind of moral collapse: chilling events were beginning to be widely reported despite official attempts to deny them. At the time that part of the Congo which concerns us here was in a unique constitutional position. From 1886 until 1908 the Congo Free State was administered under the personal rule of Leopold II, King of the Belgians; it was his private possession, his even to bequeath in his will (Stengers and Vansina 1985, 316). After 1908 it became the Belgian Congo, and then with independence in 1960 it emerged as the modern state of Zaire.

Under Leopold the commercial potential of the Congo began to be systematically exploited in a manner that had not been seen since the days when slaves were gathered at various points on the coast of Central Africa for transport across the Atlantic. In particular, supplies of rubber were extensively tapped from trees found growing wild in the forests. The methods used by the agents of the state in cajoling Leopold's Congolese subjects into supplying latex for the markets in Antwerp were often atrocious. A quota system operated, and those unable to meet the required output were sought out, and many suffered death or mutilation, especially through having their hands severed. An estimate that in the twenty years of Leopold's rule as many as five million Congolese may have been killed (Forbath 1977, 375) is impossible to confirm and may well be excessive, but it is at least an indication of the scale of the atrocities involved. The Irishman Roger Casement recorded the horrors of the period in detail, having himself spent several lengthy periods in the Congo Free State initially in the employ of Leopold (when he also met Joseph Conrad), and later as British Consul. Publication of the Casement Report in 1904 was the immediate inspiration of the founding of the Congo Reform Association in Britain, and ultimately of the creation of branches elsewhere in Europe and in the United States. The campaigning zeal that had earlier secured the repeal of the slavery laws was turned upon Brussels and thence on Central Africa.

Such outrages occurred at a time when the comfortable intellectual conceits embodied in nineteenth-century notions of social evolution, conceits which otherwise threatened to outlive the specific theoretical framework which offered a haven, were also starting to come under general attack. The ideas embodied in the image of the Dark Continent may have served to cloak some of the excesses taking place in the Congo State in a confused tangle of disregard – it would not do in Belgium, but it might be quietly overlooked in Central Africa. Yet the very fact that, once generally known, the events were widely represented as outrageous is already an indication of the beginnings of a significant drift away from the moral certitudes of nineteenth-century European engagement with Africa.

The presiding tendency in social theory had been to describe human cultures in terms of a continuum running from the least to the most evolved; those structurally and, many would have argued, chronologically more advanced had by implication a monopoly on occupancy of the high moral ground. From this vantage point there were certainly potentially awkward clouds to be seen lurking on the horizon. For instance, in scanning 'primitive' cultures it was often hard to divert attention from the fact that there appeared to be many reverberations of contemporary 'civilised' life evident: the break between the 'savage' and the 'advanced' was not completely clear-cut. E.B. Tylor, who came to occupy the first Readership in Anthropology in Britain (created at the University of Oxford in 1884), was the main proponent of one of the more successful explanations of this potentially disturbing observation. This was the idea of 'survivals'. Such reverberations were inevitable because, Tylor assured his readers (1871),

Mwene Putu Kasongo, the *kyambvu* (or king) of the Yaka. He was arrested by the Congo authorities in 1906 on what Torday regarded as a misunderstanding by government officials.

The skulls of Chokwe killed in battle as displayed by their enemies.

advanced societies retained vestiges of their primitive beginnings, relics surviving beneath the surface. Characteristically, these survivals were thought of as inert, like an archaeological find, rather than niggling and invasive like a psychological condition. They could thus be simultaneously explained, and explained away.

The aptness of the figure of Kurtz that Conrad drew and the response to the events carried out in the Congo in the name of civilised commerce suggest that for many this was becoming a debatable standpoint by the turn of the century. If certain moral and spiritual conditions were relics, they still retained their sharpness. Confidence that the story of human development displayed consistent and unwavering progress towards the good was beginning to wane; and the Congo, both in reality, and as the most characteristic home of the metaphorical image of Darkness, was a leading stage on which the expressions of this emergent intellectual doubt were starting to be played out.

Yet the period was not without its positive aspects. If the more polemical were later to characterise aspects of Victorian social thought as a kind of darkness, it was only by comparison with what could be portrayed as emerging enlightenment. The opening decade of the century was a transitional one in the human sciences. In psychology the introspective methods of the Victorian era and the concentration on the intellectual aspects of the mind which these sustained were giving way to a new emphasis on the irrational and instinctive sources of mental activity. There was increasing discussion of conation, of hidden 'drives' and, once Freud's work became more generally known, of the unconscious. What was once a subject for personal speculation was becoming a matter for the laboratory and the clinic. In Britain and Germany experimental methods were beginning to be applied to the analysis of mental events – physiology and biology, rather than metaphysical philosophy, were the new allies of psychology.

In social theory too it was a period of change. James Frazer's *The Golden Bough* came out originally in 1890 and was an immediate and immense publishing success. An enlarged edition was issued in 1900. Yet by then the first serious stirrings of disquiet over the methods and conclusions of nineteenth-century social evolutionists, endorsed from his armchair by Frazer, were beginning to become evident, and new perspectives and analytic procedures were starting to be actively canvassed. The language of social theory was gradually to shift from that of 'evolution' to that of 'history', and its intention no longer the speculative investigation of the past but something altogether more concrete – the more certifiable events of man's past. With the attention to actual events ethnography became a much more rigorous and scientific venture. Evidence was no longer sought for the exemplification of a thesis but for the construction of one. The position of the social theorist as a reflective ivory-towered scholar was increasingly being undermined.

In fact the writing had been on the wall for some time. As long ago as 1854 Richard Cull, then Secretary of the Ethnological Society, had prefaced the publication of an edition of the organisation's questionnaire by explaining: 'We are seeking facts and not inferences; what is observed

Torday in Central Africa with some of his pets.

and not what is thought' (as quoted in Urry 1972, 46). The statement and the manual were intended for the guidance of those with the opportunity to travel amongst and observe non-European cultures. By the turn of the century there were increasing numbers of scientifically inclined people who had witnessed the conditions of non-European societies for themselves, not just commissioned answers to questionnaires or read of them in the causal reports of missionaries, government agents or travellers. The new figures were technicians more interested in social and historical processes, in detailed accurate description, than tyros of philosophical method adept in articulating the sweep of theoretical ideas.

Emil Torday (1875–1931)

The immediate subject of this book and the exhibition it accompanies is one such person, Emil Torday, the Hungarian ethnographer. Torday's work was centred in the Congo State and spans virtually the whole of the relevant period, the opening decade of the century.

Torday was born in 1875, and was educated both in Hungary and Germany. On leaving Munich University, which he did before completing his degree, he moved to Belgium where he was employed for several years in a clerical position in a Brussels bank. Here he developed an interest in Leopold's distant territories in Central Africa which was to be his major preoccupation for the rest of his life. Torday left Europe as the new century dawned arriving at the mouth of the River Congo in March 1900. By the end of the year he had secured a post in Leopold's administration in the far south-eastern corner of the country near Lake Mweru. He kept no diary and made no systematic observations of an ethnographic kind, but he was interested in indigenous culture and had plenty of time to ease himself into life in an isolated area in the very centre of the continent.

Torday's official position was to a degree a nominal one. The province of Katanga (the contemporary Shaba) lay at the limits of Leopold's empire, and there were constant fears of British incursions from the neighbouring regions of Northern Rhodesia (now Zambia). Torday was appointed more or less as a token of occupation, with little in the way of formal duties. He occupied himself in the manner of those with the leisure to indulge themselves in Africa: in adventure, exploration and hunting for big game. But he did also make considerable headway in learning local languages, and found the isolation and the company of the Luba, amongst whom he mostly lived, sustaining. 'I had not the slightest desire to see Europe again, and if it had been possible I would have stayed on for the rest of my life', he later recalled (1913a, 53). His appointment, however, came to an end in 1904, and he returned to Europe on a short visit, spending time especially in Britain. It was during this trip that Torday established contact with an institution with which, though he was never an official member of its staff, he was to be closely connected for the rest of his life, the British Museum.

Subsequently Torday went to work for the Compagnie du Kasai, an independent trading company operating in the south central part of the Congo State. To start with he was based in Mbala country in the Kwango/Kwilu

Wood mask. Pende. 1910.4–20.473.
H. 21 cm.

area, and he became fluent in the local dialect, one of the fifteen languages
(eight of them African) that he was to master during his lifetime. Mbala
was sufficiently widely known that he could travel extensively in this ethni-
cally diverse region and converse with ease beyond the immediate confines
of Mbala territory. Torday began compiling ethnographic accounts of the
region and sent them back to Europe where they were published from 1905
onwards in the publications of the Anthropological Institute of Great
Britain. He also started making systematic collections of the arts of the
area and creating a photographic record. By 1906, when he resigned from
the Compagnie du Kasai, he was already being consulted as an established
authority on Congolese ethnography. Sir H.H. Johnston, for instance, used
some of Torday's field photographs, illustrations of objects he had collected,
and general ethographic and linguistic information provided by Torday
in writing his two-volume study *George Grenfell and the Congo* (1908).
Torday had also had published four significant articles and others were
in the press; and a variety of museums, especially in Britain, had benefited
from his collecting activities.

The immediate cause of Torday's decision to resign his post was an
ethical issue. The means of coercing local populations in the area into the
required kinds of commercial activity that the concessionaire firms were
operating as elsewhere was to establish *capitas*, or sentries composed of
African auxiliary forces, in each village. Their task was clear-cut: to over-
come, by whatever means, the resistance of local labour to undertaking
the expected tasks. Insurrection was common, and the disruption caused
to indigenous productive activities meant that crops were not planted out
at the appropriate time and food shortages became endemic. The Kuba,
in the Kasai region, rebelled as early as 1904, and the Compagnie du Kasai
continued to be a focus of discontent throughout the period.

Torday was a consistent apologist for the indigenous cause. Of his decision to leave the employ of the Kasai Company he later wrote that quite
simply 'news from Europe' obliged his return from Central Africa (1913a,

267). His letters, however, tell a different story. In consequence of his ethnographical work and his championing of local Congolese interests he had come to be regarded by his employers as an 'English spy'. He wrote from Kikwit in Mbala country in December 1906 to explain:

> ... since it is known that I am writing for an English revue and have sent ethnographical objects to the B.M. instead of Tervuren [now the home of the Musée Royal de l'Afrique Centrale in Belgium], I have continuel [*sic*] trouble. As further I have sent an agent to the Director (ceci entre-nous!) who has murdered natives and he, instead of giving him up to Justice, has sent him simply to Europe, neither my self-respect nor my honour have permitted me to continue here any longer.

By early 1907 he was back in Europe, for only his second brief visit since first going to Africa, and looking for a post in a British colonial territory. He was persuaded differently.

In September of that year he was once more aboard the S.S. *Bruxellesville* and bound for the Congo State. He returned, however, with a new role in view. Until this point he had worked in the field alone and as a sideline to more formal, though at times none too serious, administrative duties. Now, in the manner of the times, he was leading an expedition and had no official governmental or commercial role. His aims were directly and exclusively those of fieldwork. Apart from Torday there were initially three other members of the group, one of whom, Iredell, thought better of his inclusion whilst still aboard and disembarked on arrival in the Congo estuary. It was thus in the company of Norman Hardy, a painter of ethnographic subjects, and W.H. Hilton-Simpson, a writer, explorer and photographer with experience in North Africa, that Torday arrived again at the mouth of the River Congo.

Over the next two years the expedition sought to create a comprehensive ethnographic account of the peoples living across the southern reaches of the Equatorial Forest, concentrating, though not to the exclusion of a further foray into the Kwango/Kwilu region, on areas Torday had not already visited. The published results remain primary sources on many of the cultures described. At the same time the collection of objects formed is arguably unequalled amongst those from Central Africa in the coverage it provides of the art and material culture of the whole region lying along the southern fringes of the Equatorial Forest. By modern standards the quality of Torday's documentation of objects has its limitations. Much was left to be amplified by subsequent research. For the time, however, Torday's efforts were exceptional.

The bulk of Torday's collection is now in the British Museum where it provides a baseline from which to discuss artistic and cultural developments in those areas throughout the rest of the century. Other material went to the Pitt Rivers Museum in Oxford and to the Wellcome collection, later the Wellcome Historical Medical Museum in Euston Road, London. As much of this large holding was subsequently redistributed amongst a whole variety of public collections, Torday material has ended up in museums throughout Britain and in the United States (at the Museum of Cultural History, Los Angeles, for instance). Torday also had his own collection, parts of which went to the Hungarian Ethnographical Museum in Budapest and parts to the University Museum, Philadelphia. Finally, Hilton-Simpson also formed a collection whilst working with Torday, and this is now in the Powell Cotton Museum, Birchington-on-Sea, Kent.

Bushcraft and scholarship

During the whole of this period, and indeed until the end of his life, Torday had no formal connection with any teaching institution. He formed no 'school', had no followers or pupils, and did not even unequivocally identify himself with any of the entrenched theoretical positions that were to emerge in the 1920s and early 30s. He did, however, establish an enduring relation with the British Museum. T.A. Joyce, the curator then recently appointed to take charge of the ethnographical collections, became a firm friend and to begin with acted in a sense as Torday's amanuensis: much of the material published appeared under their joint names.

The establishment of a working relationship of that sort was also pivotal in the intellectual history of the time. Ethnography-by-letter has its own history. Tylor, for instance, received much first-hand information on Australian Aboriginal life from the missionary Lorimer Fison, whilst Frazer numbered amongst his correspondents John Roscoe, who in his own right wrote extensive monographs on Ugandan ethnography, and Baldwin Spencer, co-author (with F.J. Gillen) of the classic *The Native Tribes of Central Australia* (1899). At the prompting of his mentors in the British Museum Torday gradually transformed himself from an untrained and unsystematic observer into a detailed and precise recorder of cultural data. This he sent back from the frontline in the form of letters and lengthy pencil-written notes to be redrafted by Joyce in the comfort of the Museum library for eventual publication in a form appropriate to prevailing academic conventions.

As an arrangement this was a kind of half-way house. The collection of data and the reflection on its significance were still separate tasks carried out by two different kinds of people: the experienced expert in bushcraft on the one hand, and the scholar-curator on the other. But at least now they were co-operating closely together on a joint project with a single aim, that of accurate 'objective' documentation acquired for its own sake, rather than as further scaffolding to be erected around some pre-existing theoretical edifice.

Inevitably both Torday and Joyce were to develop their separate interests in due course, though they continued to publish ethnographical descriptions of Central Africa under their joint names until as late as 1922. Joyce, however, was by then on the brink of undertaking his own fieldwork, as an archaeologist in an area on which he had already published extensively in his own right (1912, 1914, 1916), that of South and Central American antiquity. Because of his close association with Torday some have assumed Joyce must have accompanied him in the field. Indeed, he had originally wanted to take part in the 1907 expedition but was prevented from doing so by his Museum and domestic commitments. It was not, therefore, until

Wood cup. Identified by Torday under a joint appellation, Wongo and Lele. 1910.4–20.5. H. 17 cm.

1926 that he became involved in firsthand fieldwork leading four archaeological expeditions to British Honduras between then and 1931 and
adding substantial basic materials to the British Museum's Mayan holdings
(Carmichael 1973).

Torday for his part was gradually to move in the opposite direction,
from the field to the study. To give an indication of how complete was
the switch in direction in Torday's interests it need only be mentioned
that his last published book (1930a) was a massive compilation of existing
sources of African ethnography, ironically issued as a volume in the
Descriptive Sociology series, originally devised by one of the parents of the
doctrine of social evolution, Herbert Spencer. This encyclopedic venture
followed on from a series of important and more theoretically inclined
articles on such subjects as fetishism (1929h) and dualism (1928b). These
drew on his extensive knowledge, both first and secondhand, of African
ethnography in general, and gave an Africanist perspective to issues that
were being debated in the anthropological journals often by Oceanic
specialists.

It was not that once the collaboration between Torday and Joyce on
Central Africa was advanced they began to take off in different directions.
Their starting-points were so different that in moving in opposite directions
they ended up at roughly the same point: even though Joyce's interests
were to a degree also archaeological, he, like Torday, sought to link the
insights of firsthand observation with established traditions of scholarship
and to transform them in the process. Put simply, the trajectory of their
two interrelated careers illustrates well the alternative routes by which
the distinctive emphasis in British anthropology, that of field-based speculation, came about.

That Torday, a Central European, should have been a part of this process
in Britain is certainly a curious circumstance. Yet he was not unique in
this amongst anthropologists in the English-speaking world. It was, after
all, Malinowski, a Pole, who was to occupy centre stage in the polemics
surrounding the development of British anthropological method in the
1920s and 30s (and, for that matter, Conrad, also of Polish descent, who
emerged as the leading literary figure of his generation writing in English).
Torday and Malinowski knew each other and each other's work. Indeed,
at Torday's death Malinowski paid his Central European colleague an
eloquent tribute. Torday, he said, was 'one of the world's foremost anthropologists ... His ability to reach the personal element in Africans, and
to gain their affection, as well as his sure grasp of theoretical problems
placed him among the makers of modern ethnology' (1931).

Malinowski was never prone to understatement in his opinions on the
qualities of fellow anthropologists, whether in praise or denunciation –
a habit of mind he shared with Torday. However, his gifts were not those
of prophecy and in spite of this high opinion Torday has subsequently been
seen as only a footnote, if that, to the history of his chosen subject. He
now never receives even a mention in what is becoming a burgeoning
literature on the development of anthropology in the opening decades of
the century. Langham (1981), Stocking (1983), and Urry (1972, 1984),

to mention only a few of the most immediate and recent sources, do not discuss his contribution at all; whilst Penniman, writing a history of the anthropology of the period just four years after Torday's death, mentions Torday as only a secondary source on another Africanist, the celebrated seventeenth-century Dutch traveller Olfert Dapper (1935, 37). Yet, if Torday has been neglected by all but those with specific interests in the cultures and peoples amongst whom he worked, he remains a compelling exemplar of the currents at work at the time.

The Kuba collection

The collection Torday formed was only one product of his travels in the Congo State. Indeed, it is arguable that – as with Malinowski, another benefactor of the British Museum – the proper light in which to regard Torday's work is as that of a field anthropologist rather than a field collector of ethnographic objects or of art. The important contribution Torday made to the consideration of the whole art and culture history of what is now southern Zaire derives from his passionate interest in creating an objective, documentary record. As he wrote from the field to Hercules Read, Head of the Department in which Joyce worked, 'I have not chosen objects for their beauty but for the interest they may have for the anthropologist and I hope that in this I have acted for the best' (19 November 1905).

This sounds like an early endorsement of an assumption which persists even today, and continues to be debated with considerably more heat than light, that an anthropological approach in some way constitutes a denial of aesthetic interests. It sometimes seems to be assumed that anthropologists are trained rigorously to erase all private perceptions of quality from the consideration of objects, just as personal preference and prejudice should be excluded from the formation of the ethographic record. Such curious acts of self-denial, however, are quite at odds with the restless awkward questioning which is otherwise held to be characteristic of anthropological method. In the end Torday too was led to adopt a more personal, engaged style in his ethnographic work. He could hardly do otherwise since he so clearly enjoyed the interactive aspect of fieldwork; and the same is true of the artefacts he acquired. It is as if suspension of judgement was an appropriate strategy in the face of a prevailing opinion of Congolese that tended to be condemnatory; once, however, something so singularly impressive as to invite only positive response was encountered, the protective curtain of scientific distance could be drawn back and facts allowed to speak for themselves.

For Torday Kuba art and culture, which he came to know during his last expedition, invited such an unveiling. 'Have the staff of police at the Museum been doubled to keep out the publishers?', he enquired of Joyce (8 March 1909), anticipating great public interest in his account of the Kuba and in the objects he was collecting. 'If it [the Kuba collection] gets lost on the way', he wrote on another occasion, 'I blow my brains out' (30 June 1908). The Museum authorities also agreed that the qualities of this part of the collection were exceptional, and a selection of objects was immediately placed on display in a special case in the Ethnography

Wood figure (*ndop*) commemorating the founder of the Kuba kingdom, Shyaam aMbul aNgoong. The image at the front of the plinth on which he sits is a game board, an object which he is reported in oral traditions to have introduced among the Kuba. Kuba-Bushoong. 1909.12–10.1. H. 54.5 cm. (Collected at Nsheng, the Kuba capital; see also *cover*.)

Galleries where *The Times* advised its readers the art of 'one of the most remarkable tribes of Africa' (16 August 1909) was to be seen.

Within the whole of the Torday collections (which runs to nearly 3,000 pieces in the British Museum alone) three objects were outstanding. These were representations of Kuba kings, including that commemorating the founder of the ruling dynasty, Shyaam aMbul aNgoong (or Shamba Bolongongo in Torday's orthography). To Torday they seemed (wrongly as it happens) like portraits done from life, as would be appropriate in a society where kingship itself was revered. The figures appeared the very embodiment of the legitimacy of royal power. Unlike so many of the objects Torday had documented, these appeared to have been deliberately preserved, even treasured. Indeed, Torday's own account, confirmed by the independent witness of Hilton-Simpson, suggests that it was precisely because the king and his court were impressed with the image presented to them of the British Museum as a treasury of the finest in world cultures that they were willing to dispose of these examples and a fourth which was given to Torday as a leaving present.

In style and conception the figures were eminently accessible to European taste – rounded and naturalistic, not angular or resistant to interpretation like the African sculpture that was just beginning to be appreciated in the more innovative studios in Paris. When the figures were put on display it was with the photographic image of the king whom Torday had known, and for whom he had an immense regard, Kot aPe (or Kwete in Torday's spelling). Thus, in collapsing together two different traditions of naturalistic representation, the sculpted and the photographic portrait, Kuba history was, it seemed, updated. The refinement of which the older historic carvings appeared so eloquently to speak was carried into a contemporary world where the reputation of the citizens of the Congo State was often considerably more ambiguous.

Beyond these three specific pieces, however, the characteristics of the rest of the collection also came as a revelation. The Kuba, Torday later asserted, 'are undoubtedly the greatest artists of black Africa; as weavers, embroiderers, carvers in wood and as workers of metal they have not their equals in the whole continent; for metal work one might except the people of Benin who, however, were taught by Europeans' (1925a, 203). This

Wood box. Kuba-Ngongo.
1908.Ty41. H. 9 cm, W. 46 cm.
(Probably collected at Misumba.)

Raffia textile with cut-pile
embroidery. The colours are black
and yellow. Kuba-Shoowa.
1979.Af1.2674. w. 49 cm.
(See also *cover*.)

picture of the development of Nigerian metalworking techniques (including those of Benin) has been completely revised since Torday wrote, and the role allocated to European inspiration is now negligible. Nevertheless, the fact that in so many areas of Kuba artistic production detailed attention to surface and finish is characteristic remains an acknowledged and celebrated feature of their traditions. Mats are made only from lath and string but even so are, in Torday's assessment, 'objects of very great beauty' (p. 204). Cloth is produced from raffia, 'the coarse stuff gardeners use to tie up their plants', but even so the finished textile is as fine as 'the flimsiest linen' with all the 'suppleness of silk' (p. 205); embroidered surfaces 'remind one of the illumination of old Celtic manuscripts' (p. 208); carved objects, however humble in function, can be 'objects of art' (p. 211).

The leading feature of all these artistic products, whatever the material of which they were composed or the technique of their manufacture, is the elaborate design with which their surfaces are often covered. Each design element has its own distinguishing pattern name, and Torday copiously recorded these, illustrating his various writings on Kuba art with intricate drawings of the configurations. Whatever the appeal of such an extensive decorative tradition to the museum visitor of the time, Torday's documentation of Kuba arts was also of importance to the scientific community.

A.C. Haddon, who was a central figure in the establishment of anthropology at Cambridge University, and in the creation of ethnographic collections in the associated University Museum, had before the turn of the century called for just such an emphasis in the study of ethnographic arts (1894, 1895; see also Urry 1982). Through minute attention to the study of design would emerge, he suggested, a graphic illustration of the intricacies of evolutionary process at work in culture in general. Torday held Haddon in no great esteem; even so, his exposition of Kuba pattern was to an extent prefigured in Haddon's discussion of design in the Papuan Gulf. It too linked to a wider range of emergent interests. At Oxford Henry Balfour was developing similar interests drawing in part on Tylor's discussions of decorative art. It may be that the excitement of practising artists in Britain was no match for that shown by the avant-garde in France in non-Western art, but, arguably, the essentially scholarly and ethnographical interests that were developing were equally important to the establishment of longer-term interest in the subject. Unlike the concerns of artists in France, those of English-speaking anthropologists led to ethnographic arts being investigated on their own terms rather than simply appropriated by European art interests.

In addition to the moral and scientific senses in which Torday's work in Central Africa can be seen as contributing shape and substance to the intellectual emphasis of the new century, in the field of art studies the phrase 'patterns in the darkness' has a very direct application. The concern with pattern, which formed one strain in the history of ethnological interests, was matched by the artistic interests of the Kuba themselves. 'Prepare room for the Bakuba collection,' Torday wrote portentously to Joyce from the field, 'you will want it!' (6 March 1908).

Torday camped in a village on the River Sankuru, 1908.

2 The notebook, the questionnaire and the camera

Torday's association with the British Museum began conventionally enough. On 4 May 1904 C.H. (later Sir Hercules) Read, the Keeper of the Department of British and Medieval Antiquities and Ethnography, received a short note from Torday. For the occasion Torday used a French version of his Christian name adapted to Belgian usage in the Congo, but later dropped in favour of the original Hungarian form. The note read: 'Mr. Emile Torday presents his compliments to Mr. Read and should be thankful if Mr. Read would inform him of the time he could meet him in the Museum. Mr. Torday wishes to give some trifle curioes [sic] of Central Africa (Baluba country) to the British Museum and ask Mr. Read's advise [sic] for others'. A week later he came in by arrangement and presented the Museum with thirty-eight pieces from the south-eastern Congo. Towards the end of the year he donated a further four objects.

Wood mask. Luba. 1909.Ty1022.
H. 48 cm. (Collected at Banagasu.)

The 'trifle curioes' were somewhat oddly documented – a thumb piano collected by Torday before it had been completed was described as being 'used by Baluba bakers in making bread', and an example of a *lubuko*, an object used in divination, was said to be a 'snuff-grinder'. Torday was at that point little more than an enthusiastic amateur, an adventurer employed as a rather eccentric colonial official in the remote south-eastern corner of the Congo Free State. When in Brussels he had eagerly read all he could on the Congo for which he had conceived a passionate interest. He had already attended courses at the University of Munich but had not been instructed in anthropology – and in his four years in Africa he had kept no systematic record of an ethnographic kind, nor a diary. Indeed, Torday's literary output at that point was limited to his part in the founding of a small newspaper whilst in Kinshasa awaiting an appointment; and that may not have been an entirely serious affair: it was called *Le Petit Leopoldvillain*, and the subscription was a case of forty-eight bottles of beer per annum which was retained for the edification of the editorial staff (Torday 1913a, 21). Nevertheless, when Torday returned to Central Africa in February 1905 he had reached a special understanding with the authorities of the British Museum. Indeed, though disbarred as a Hungarian citizen from holding any formal position, he had, in a sense, become an agent of the Museum; and, as the relationship developed, its Trustees were later to write on his behalf to seek exemption from normal customs procedures in the Congo so that he could formally collect on behalf of the Museum. By then they had agreed to lend support to a further long-term expedition Torday was to propose.

One of the first questions these circumstances raise is how it could be that this degree of co-operation with an unknown Hungarian, in the employ of Belgian interests, and undertaking his first visit to Britain, can have come about. Certainly, field ethnography, then as now, can be an expensive business. The difference between the cost of a stamp to solicit information from someone already on the spot and that of maintaining an expedition in the field for lengthy periods of time, could be compelling enough a calculation to keep the scholars in their armchairs. Someone of competence and reliability willing to act on their behalf as a sideline to other forms of employment had obvious attraction. Yet, however impressive Torday may have seemed to the Museum's curators – and he never lacked confidence in his own abilities – we need to look beyond his persuasiveness, his obvious aptitude and appetite for the task, for a fuller explanation.

The Torres Straits precedent

The first professional anthropologist to form an association with the British Museum was Alfred C. Haddon. It is true that at the time he was in fact Professor of Zoology at the Royal College of Science in Dublin, a post which he held in tandem with that of Assistant Naturalist at the Science and Art Museum. Yet, in 1888, whilst working officially as a marine biologist on a study of the reef systems in the Torres Straits (lying between Australia and New Guinea), Haddon had begun to record anthropological information and had formed an important ethnographic collection (Moore 1984). On his return he set about arranging the material in the British Museum's galleries (Quiggan 1942, 92), and the collection was subsequently acquired together with detailed ethnographic information on each object. The quality and range of this documentation set a precedent which Torday himself was to follow.

Haddon, however, was not simply a forerunner in museological terms. Whatever the claims to priority later made by Malinowski, a second Torres Straits expedition organised by Haddon in 1898 arguably provides the best place at which to start recounting the distinctive emphasis on the firsthand experience of another culture which has so frequently been cited as characteristic of British anthropology. Haddon's conversion from zoology to anthropology was already well advanced (Urry 1982). He had moved from Dublin to Cambridge where he was appointed to teach physical anthropology, a commitment he initially overlapped with his Professorship in Ireland. The 1898 expedition provided the springboard for a decisive shift into the cultural aspects of the emergent discipline.

The occasion also provided an introduction to 'live' ethnography for several others who were to become influential figures in the history of anthropology in Britain, and led to their following the same route as Haddon from the natural to the human sciences. The most important convert of all was W.H.R. Rivers, then an experimental psychologist with a specialist interest in the physiology and functioning of the sense organs, especially vision. Rivers was to emerge as the leading anthropologist of his generation (Langham 1981; Mack 1975; Slobodin 1978); at first, however, he turned down Haddon's invitation to join the expedition. Only when two of his own most talented students, C.S. Myers (included in part because of his musical knowledge) and William McDougal, subsequently accepted, did he change his mind. Similarly, C.G. Seligman, later well known to Africanists for his anthropological surveys in Sudan (1932) written with his wife (who is also known to the British Museum as the source of the famous Benin ivory mask), went to the Torres Straits as a trained pathologist with the aim of studying native health and medical practice. The expedition membership was completed by a linguist, Sydney Ray, and a young undergraduate engaged as photographer, Anthony Wilkin.

At first sight the outcome of the Torres Straits work looks impressive. The published results came out in six substantial volumes which appeared between 1902 and 1935 under Haddon's general editorship. This second expedition also yielded an even larger ethnographic collection which this time went mostly to the Cambridge University Museum of Archaeology and Anthropology. No doubt from the privileged standpoint of contemporary practice there is a lot that looks superficial even in these achievements. Indeed, scarcely before the first volume of Expedition Reports was out Haddon himself was recommending a much more intensive version of field research which adopted a comprehensive approach within a limited area or group of related peoples (1903, 22). Of the Torres Straits participants Rivers had in fact already done just that, having spent an extended period in 1901–2 working on his own amongst the Toda of the Nilgiri Hills in

Wood figure, described as a 'house charm'. Kuba-Ngende. 1908.Ty164. H. 29 cm.

Wood hairpin. Pende.
1910.4– 20.461.
H. 21 cm.

southern India (Rivers 1906). Yet the way the Torres Straits expedition was organised had precluded this more intensive method of investigation. This had been survey work; it was an 'expedition', with the participants to an extent hunting information down in packs and obviating the possibility of more direct personal relationships developing with their 'informants'. They also worked exclusively in pidgin English. The significance of this phase in British anthropology, however, lies not in any deficiencies revealed in these details of method but in the fact that a group of scientists should be in the field at all – and that the limitations of the conditions of their being there should have been so readily recognised.

Museums and anthropologists

It might seem that the backgrounds of the personnel in the department of the British Museum dealing with ethnography at the time represented a different, and an older, strain of interest in the subject. The division between them and the new scientifically orientated discipline seems to mirror that between, for example, Sir James Frazer – popular, scholarly and respected, but yesterday's man – and, say, Rivers, the serious dedicated scientist setting down an agenda for the future. For a start none of the British Museum curators could claim a scientific education. Within the British Museum structural reorganisation had already taken Natural History off to occupy a separate site in South Kensington; ethnography remained within the context of an antiquities department. Inevitably curators were recruited from the ranks of those with broad antiquarian and classical interests.

C.H. Read had come into the British Museum at a young age under the patronage of A.W. Franks. He was to an extent trained on the job through the unrivalled resources of the Museum department to which he was attached, and he acquired (Braunholtz 1970) a remarkable knowledge of the whole range of antiquities of which he became principal custodian in 1896. Enthnography was only one of these, and although Read was to become President of the Anthropological Institute (later the Royal Anthropological Institute) twice (in the period 1899–1901 and again from 1917 to 1919) and was President of Section H (the Anthropology Section) of the British Association for the Advancement of Science in 1898, he published sparsely in the field (1891). Certainly he undertook no fieldwork. The year before Read's elevation to the Keepership O.M. Dalton, an Oxford classicist, was added to the staff. In 1902 Read himself sought someone to specialise in the developing ethnographic holdings and to see into print a *Handbook* to the collection, a project already begun by Dalton (the first edition being published in 1910). For the first time candidates were required to have passed an examination in Anthropology (Haddon 1903, 20). Thomas Athol Joyce, the successful candidate, was another Oxford-trained classicist; H.J. Braunholtz, appointed as Joyce's assistant in 1913, was a Cambridge classicist; and even so distinguished a recent Keeper of Enthnography as William Fagg also had a classical background (though Adrian Digby, appointed in 1932, had by then already become the first anthropologist trained as such to join the British Museum).

'Samuel K. Bay Esq. Gent', one of Torday's entourage during his 1907–9 expedition with W.M. Hilton-Simpson.

It would be too simplistic, however, to characterise classical interests as an impediment to participating at the cutting edge of the developing science of anthropology – though, interestingly, when Joyce went to the field in the late 1920s it was to work on a 'classical' subject, Mayan archaeology, and not straight ethnography. Arguably, museums and universities should be seen as two different sorts of institution. It was not that museums provided a safe haven for the intellectually conservative and universities gave succour to the innovative insights of men from the natural sciences; the essential role the Museum sought to perform was to act as a resource: it had a built-in antiquarian slant. Of course, in the 1890s the Museum and the learned societies to which it was linked had been virtually the only resources of this kind. Anthropology barely existed in the universities. Indeed, in the wake of the Torres Straits expedition it was still a decade before the universities were producing trained field-workers. And when they did, a number, not least Malinowski, were to form further field collections for the British Museum, endorsing its role as both an academic and a public resource.

There was no competition between converts from the classics and those from the natural sciences, or between museum-based and university-based anthropology. Haddon, for one, had feet in both camps; and Haddon like all his contemporaries was still working to improve on the model of social

Described as a 'hunting fetish' (*tembo*), this wood figure has copper strips on the eyes, nose and forehead and is encircled with lengths of creeper. Kuba-Ngongo. 1908.Ty148. H. 48 cm. (Collected at Misumba.)

Crocodile jaw, the upper surface shaved flat, and with a wood disc. The instrument is used in divination by rubbing the disc up and down whilst the diviner repeats a series of possible causes of misfortune or solutions. When the disc stops the oracle has pronounced. Kuba-Bushoong. 1909.5–13.316. (Collected at Nsheng.)

evolution rather than any more radical programme leading to its overthrow as a guiding paradigm. Furthermore, there is no doubt that from a museological point of view the increasing precision in field method and the formation of systemic collections of material culture which Haddon had pioneered were welcome developments with which curators kept in touch. Through intermediate organisations such as the Anthropological Institute (whose home was then opposite the front gates of the British Museum) secure links were maintained with the developing science. Thus Joyce, for instance, continued a tradition of Museum involvement in the Institute's affairs begun by A.W. Franks and Read in acting as Editor

Torday's dog and phonograph.

Benin material, and even had the co-operation of the German Consul-General in Nigeria in negotiating with followers of the fugitive Oba of Benin to obtain any specimens that he might have carried off with him as he fled before the British troops. When Dalton sought to prepare a catalogue of Benin material (Read and Dalton 1899), he was obliged to visit Germany in order to look particularly at ivories and bronze heads of which he found up to eight times more specimens in Berlin. His report on his visit, in the form of a letter to Hercules Read from which the information above is derived, was published officially – itself an unusual move – by Her Majesty's Stationery Office (1898) and contains a salutary commentary on the difference between the financial and organisational state of German and British museums. In terms of the size of its ethnographical collections he found that Berlin 'has no rivals . . . On a moderate estimate the Berlin collections are six or seven times as extensive as ours. To mention a single point, the British Province of Assam is represented in Berlin by a whole room, and in London by a single case' (1898, 7). The fact that German institutions should be so well represented in areas of British interest seemed especially galling.

The point did not go unnoticed in anthropological circles. Thus Northcote Thomas, a close ally of Joyce and friend of Torday, was overall Editor of a monograph series on 'The Native Races of the British Empire'. The volume on British Central Africa issued in 1906 (under the authorship of Alice Werner) contained a preface by Northcote Thomas which restated Dalton's concern in more polemical form. The reported gap had also widened since Dalton's estimate:

> In twenty-five years the Berlin Museum has accumulated
> ethnographical collections more than ten times as large as those of the
> British Museum, and the work of collection goes on incessantly . . . If,
> one hundred years hence, English anthropologists have to go to
> Germany to study the remains of those who were once our subject
> races, we shall owe this humiliation to the supineness of England at
> the end of the nineteenth and early twentieth century. The past, once
> lost, can never be recovered . . .

Alice Werner herself told the African Society several years later that Torday's work in association with the British Museum was 'almost, if not quite, the most important work done in anthropology since the opening of the century' (1910, 206). In fact, the major British work of the decade, in the wake of the anthropological initiation of the Torres Straits group, was being undertaken prinicipally in Oceania. Islands, in Haddon's view, were particularly important to investigate as here the incursions of outside influence were more rapidly corrupting 'traditional' patterns of culture than elsewhere. In Africa, however, whatever challenge German museum policy posed was most acute. In the light of the history of the acquisition of the Benin collections Torday was to write from the field to reassure Joyce that 'although dear Frobenius says that he had got everything still obtainable and that he left nothing for people to come after him, I think I have done well and that the old curiosity shop of Bloomsbury may still take

Tetela-Sungu woman, one of a number of paintings Torday had done by Norman Hardy to illustrate styles of body decoration. A thorough photographic record of styles of scarification was also made on the various expeditions.

its place with the Great Berlin Museum' (15 April 1908). He struck a note that might have been too shrill for official British Museum politesse but one which was none the less resonant.

Aids to observation

No detailed account remains of what took place at any of the 'foregatherings' between Read, Joyce and Torday in the second half of 1904. One solid outcome, however, does survive. This is the *Questionnaire Ethnographique* (1905), a specially adapted version written in French for residents of the Congo of the familiar *Notes and Queries in Anthropology*, the companion of residents and serious travellers to remote places, which had first been published in 1874. Northcote Thomas, as a member of the Council of the Anthropological Institute, helped the other three in drafting the questionnaire, which was published through the Belgian Institut de Sociologie in Brussels. One hundred copies were distributed to officials in the Congo State and to residents such as missionaries with an invitation to respond directly either to Torday – described on the brochure as 'explorateur du Congo' – at Dima, the headquarters of the Kasai Company, or to Read at the British Museum. In other words, although Torday used the questionnaire as a guide in his own work, and Joyce used it as a checklist of topics in organising Torday's fieldnotes, it was also intended as a device by which to get the machinery of the incipient colonial administration functioning to the general benefit of the project.

As a document it is comprehensive, covering 65 subjects in 24 pages with the largest number of questions (46) devoted to Religion and with but a single question on Inventions. The emphasis on religion is in part a reflection of the balance of interests in *Notes and Queries* as it had been devised under the supervision of Tylor, and also perhaps represents an attempt to refine the information that might come from mission sources. The fact, however, that so many questions were grouped under the heading of Religion is also misleading, for it was treated as a single undifferentiated subject. In practice, art and material culture were the general subjects of the first set of over twenty topics which sought information down to such details as the intricacies of rope-making, or the amount, character and place on the body of scarification with admonitions to record variations by sex and by social class and to note whether the appropriate markings were reproduced on sculpted images or not. To that extent, though material culture concerns had been a part of other questionnaires, there was some museological bias in the questions asked. However, the document was also designed with an eye for the more sophisticated problems of a non-material kind being raised by contemporary anthropology.

The previous edition of *Notes and Queries* had been published in 1899 – the year the Torres Straits expedition returned and too early to incorporate the experiences of that venture. It is one index of the links of the authors of the questionnaire with the intellectual and scientific community outide the museum world that they should have incorporated a set of instructions to respondents that relate directly to the main issues of the moment. Thus, the longest question prepared was in the section of kinship

Kwilu villagers listening to Torday's phonograph.

(section XXXIX) and dealt with the collection of genealogies. Shortly after his return Rivers had outlined one of the major theoretical findings of his research in the Torres Straits, the genealogical method (Rivers 1900). Genealogies, it was suggested, are not merely personal or family records but a kind of hieroglyphics in which is written a codified history of many social institutions. They are concrete social documents which reflect the centrality of kin relationships in social organisation generally. Here, therefore, the questionnaire departed from the usual procedure to give details not only of what questions should be asked but of how they should be asked, and of how the information should be recorded. Respondents were warned of the dangers of using imprecise categories such as 'uncle' or 'cousin', of the possibility that different terms might be used in speaking of, rather than to, relatives, or that terminology might differ between the sexes. They were invited to go on to enquire into rules of avoidance between kin and rules of residence, and to use genealogy to investigate clan structure. Subsequent sections pose another set of related questions on systems of marriage and on the family.

To be in a position to answer all these questions suggests a quality of engagement in indigenous affairs and a level of professionalism that far exceed what casual observation would imply. In an introductory note Read warned that a degree of 'intimacy' would be essential if anything satisfactory was to be learnt concerning systems of belief. Indeed, even phrasing the right questions, finding appropriate vocabulary in native languages through which to explore concepts, would be difficult. No doubt the know-ledge that Torday himself was to be one of the main users of the manual permitted this degree of elaboration in its detail and content.

The questionnaire, of course, was essentially an aid to fact gathering, a control to regulate which kind of information was recorded, a dispassion-ate document devised to render observation as 'objective' as possible. The facts should be pristine, untainted by personal opinion or judgement as scientific tradition dictated. When Torday set sail from Southampton on 11 February 1905, he also had two other instruments of objectivity in his luggage: one was his camera, the other a phonograph.

Torday is unlikely to go down in the annals of photography as a signifi-cant practitioner (Mack 1989); many of the photographs he subsequently published had to be substantially retouched to make them even passable. As he pessimistically wrote to Joyce on one occasion: 'The prints I sent will fade away, because I never can wash a photo long enough as in tepid water the gelatine dissolves. If you look well at the couple inclosed [sic] you will see the gelatine burst, not only the too big bubbles but all over the photograph' (8 March 1909). Unfortunate as this is, it does not alter the fact that Torday thought photography an important part of the ethno-graphic enterprise; and he persevered.

The photographic print is the ethnographic equivalent of the anatomical drawing – its virtue lies precisely in the fact that it deals only in givens, not in interpreting and interrogating its subject. Where many others took photographs in Africa as mementoes, outriders of impressions and events they themselves had experienced, or for any number of more popular pur-poses, Torday's aims were explicitly scientific. He rarely strayed in front of the camera himself, even when others were present to take photographs for him; rather he sought to create a cultural record as indelible and exact as a thumb-print. He did not set out to use the camera analytically but to exploit its potential as a neutral (or so it seemed), and therefore an accu-rate, instrument of description. For that reason also, although in the course of the 1907–9 expedition both Torday and his travelling companion Hilton-Simpson took photographs, they never sought to identify them-selves individually as the authors of particular shots. The subject in front of the lens was what counted, not the person behind it.

The phonograph also fitted well with the spirit of objectivity which Torday had embibed. Myers had pioneered ethnomusicology in the Torres Straits. With the phonograph Torday could record actual performance to supplement the musical instruments which were a significant element in the ethnographic collections he formed, and the texts of songs that he wrote down. The questionnaire, the camera and the phonograph were instruments of the new role which Torday had been encouraged to adopt during his short furlough in Europe, that of documentalist. Collecting objects, like making ethnographic observations, taking photographs or making recordings of song were equivalent activities. Everything was potentially valuable and should be accurately described and recorded. Torday's sentiments, as nurtured and trained by Read and Joyce, had emerged as those of the archivist.

3 The Kwilu: an ethnographic apprenticeship

Starting with the years 1905 and 1906 – the period when he was in the employ of the Kasai Company – Torday was obliged to plan his journeys and select those settlements in which he took up residence with commercial considerations in mind. He had, however, the opportunity to travel extensively through the area of the Kwango-Kwilu River Basins and approach the boundaries of the Congo State with Angola. This was the westernmost region in which he worked. From these visits derive some of the earliest authoritative reports on peoples such as the Mbala, Mbuun, Yansi, Hungaan, Kwesi, Yaka and other smaller groups in the region; the earliest scientifically documented collections of the arts of these areas were also formed at this time.

For the second expedition Torday was guided by more directly ethnographic considerations and, in particular, by the aim of researching those peoples in the southern Congo who had been least studied. He always intended during 1905–6 to visit the Kuba further to the east but had been prevented from doing so by a rebellion in the Kasai area. Paradoxically, it was only after he had left the service of the Kasai Company itself, from 1907, that he visited Kasai province. That exploration of the Kasai and adjacent areas produced material not only – most famously – on the Kuba but also on, amongst other groups, the Lele, Wongo, Tetela and Songye. Yet during this second period of Torday's association with the British Museum he was also to return to the Kwilu and revisit some of the peoples with whom he had already established relationships several years earlier. This further expedition is the subject of Chapter 4.

Such toings-and-froings disrupt the neat portrayal of Torday's progress across the southern Equatorial Forest; consideration of one area does not necessarily lead directly into that of a neighbouring one. Equally the ethnographic collections, as they arrived and were registered in the Museum were not consistently from adjacent areas; and the ethnographic reports on the people to the west of the Kasai were published in two blocks (Torday and Joyce 1905, 1906a and b, 1907a and b, and 1922; and Torday 1919), the later publications incorporating material collected on the 1907–9 expedition. Nevertheless, one consistent and progressive thread running through the narrative of these journeys is the story of Torday's own initiation in anthropology. Torday's interests were to change; he came to regard the enterprise of fieldwork differently, and, related to this, his methods and approach evolved. In parallel with an increasing confidence in the collec-

Opposite 1. Wood mask with projecting fur-lined prongs and a fibre costume attached. Tetela-Sungu, 1979.Af1.2397.
L. (including raffia costume) 142 cm.

2. A young Kuba-Ngongo man. (A painting by Norman Hardy.)

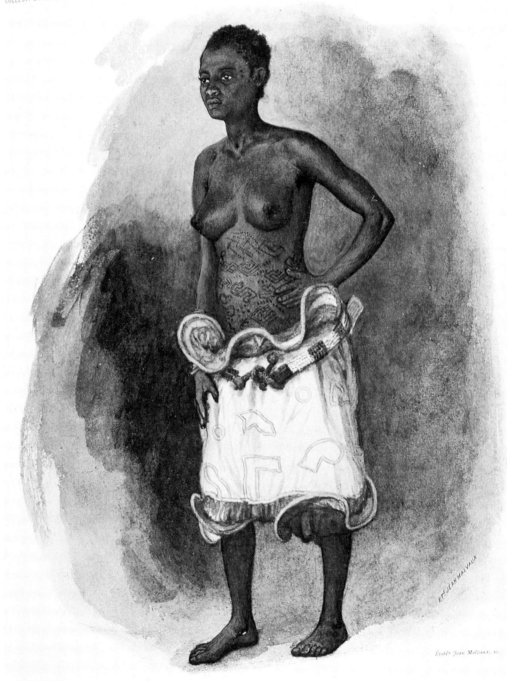

Pl. VI.

Ets JEAN MALVAUX, sc.

Établ.ts Jean Malvaux, sc.

3. High-ranking Kuba-Ngongo woman. The patterns on her skirt are appliquéd; on her abdomen are a range of designs showing styles of female scarification. (A painting by Norman Hardy.)

Left 4. Adze with a wood haft and metal blade. Such adzes were essentially for ceremonial use and carried over the shoulder by dignitaries. Wongo. 1910.4–20.78. H. 33.5 cm.

Above 5. Wood mask with fibre coiffure. Pende. 1910.4–20.476. H. 21 cm.

Above 6. Wood cup. Wongo, a
people related to the Kuba and living
to their west. 1910.4–20.2.
H. 18 cm.

Right 7. Wood cup. Wongo.
1910.4–20.21. H. 21 cm.

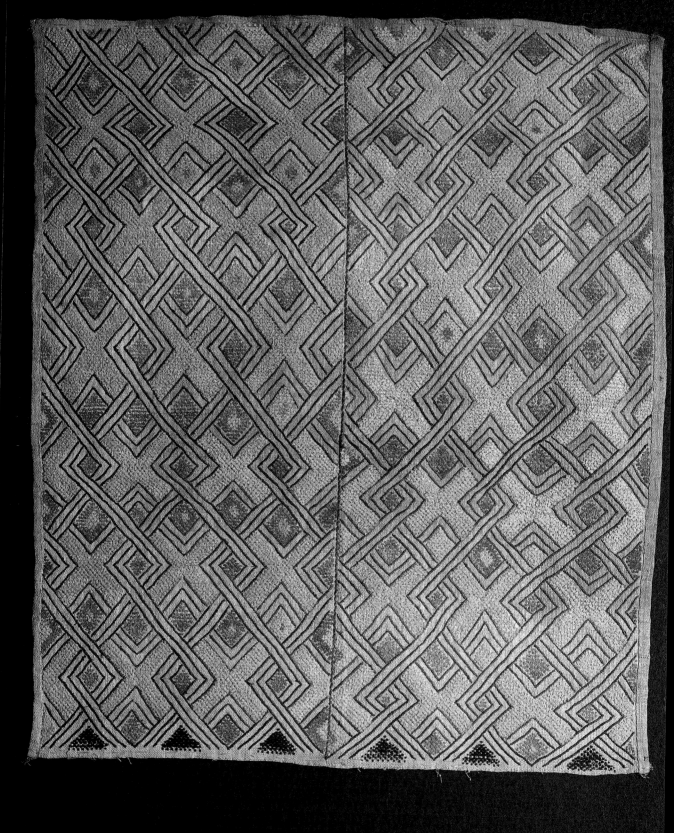

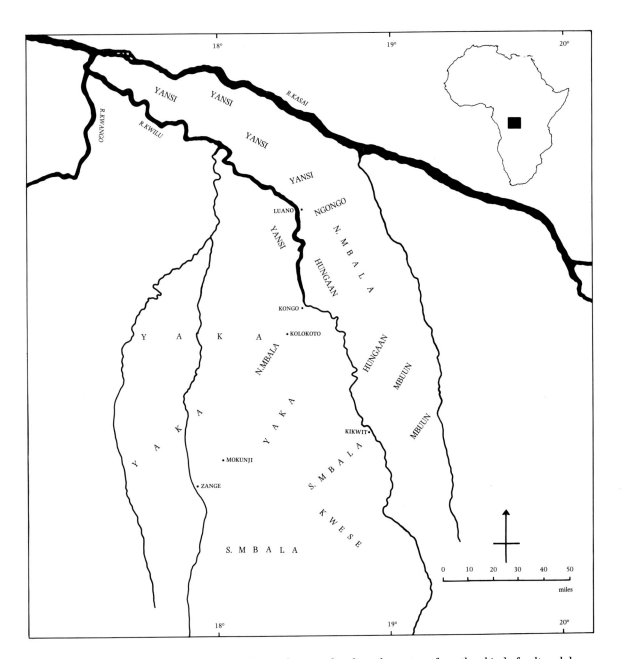

The Kwilu basin.

8. Raffia textile with cut-pile and conventional embroidery. Kuba-Ngongo. 1909.5–13.544. w. 55 cm.

tion of raw ethnographic data the status of another kind of cultural document, the museum collections of art and material culture which he was forming, was also to alter.

The northern Mbala

By 18 March 1905 Torday was already in Dima on the Kasai River and writing to inform Joyce that 'a box containing certain objects' was packed and awaiting an occasion to be sent on. Among other things it contained, according to the correspondence, a brass Nyamwezi kettle, a southern Luba stool, and an Nsapo (Zappo Zap) calabash and basketwork. None of these come from areas Torday could have visited in early 1905, suggesting they are probably the residue of his earlier sojourn in the Lake Mweru area. On 9 April he wrote further to say that a number of Pende masks were being dispatched, the second part of the collection. Again, however, these could not be field collections – there had not been time or opportunity to move into the heart of Pende country. Indeed, one of the pieces is unfinished, and nearly all have a fresh unused appearance which suggests that they were either made for commercial purposes and brought to Dima to be sold or were commissioned from an itinerant Pende carver. Fieldwork proper had not yet started.

Wood headrest, the supporting figure in Janus form. Northern Mbala. 1907.5–28.13. H. 17.5 cm. (Collected at Mossonge.)

From Dima Torday ventured south spending several months at Kongo, a river port on the Kwilu with a mixed Yansi and Hungaan population. Even here he did not begin in earnest. In the spirit of Haddon's pleas for salvage ethnography Read had warned on the front page of the questionnaire that peoples must be found whose exposure to outside influences was limited and who remained unaffected by cultural intermingling. Pristine facts could only be collected from pristine people – and there were still enough of the assumptions of social evolution around to suggest that pristine people still existed in out-of-the-way places. Torday thus had to wait until he moved to the Mbala settlement of Kolokoto, an awkward trek of over five hours from Kongo, before finding peoples in the right cultural condition to perform as subjects of ethnographic research.

Kolokoto was a small Mbala community of only 100 people, though with a larger population in the surrounding countryside; this area was to be an important point of departure for Torday. It was here that he became fluent in Kimbala and began writing up fieldnotes; and it is from here that the first parts of the field collection proper come. Indeed, when later Torday began to make a distinction between the northern and

Pende maskers. A photograph taken in 1909 on a later visit Torday made to this part of what by then had become the Belgian Congo.

Wood mask. Pende. 1910.4–20. 478. H. 12.5 cm. (Collected in 1909, and an authentic example – as may be deduced from its appearance in the adjacent field photograph.)

southern groups of the Mbala, it was often expressed in terms of the differences between the population of the area of Kolokoto and that to the south. This village and its immediate hinterland came to constitute a standard by which the rest of Mbala culture was to be judged. This was both because Torday set up residence here and because it was in Kolokoto that he recruited his main servant, who stayed with him throughout his two years in the Kwilu. This was an eight-year-old boy who, incredibly to modern ideas, used to collect basic ethnographic data for Torday and check details when people were reluctant to discuss with Torday himself. Despite his years, however, Torday declared him an invaluable assistant.

The village of Kolokoto had been established for about ten years only when Torday settled there. Its founder and ruler was Kikungulu, a wealthy man credited with extensive magical powers. If in general Torday was to act as an apologist for much in indigenous life, and frequently declared his preference for the company and good opinion of Congolese over that of Europeans charged with their administration, Kikungulu was the exception. Torday described him as 'tall and ill-favoured' (1913a, 102), avaricious and cruel. He reportedly subjected his own sister to the poison ordeal, which he administered not merely because she was suspected of being a witch but more basely, Torday suggested, so Kikungulu could obtain her money and belongings. Later Torday himself rescued the chief of a neighbouring village from being buried alive in Kolokoto, a traditional fate in cases of proven witchcraft, and took the accused into his own household. Torday, it seems, lost out all round: the man proved a most ungrateful and demanding guest who was subsequently killed anyway, and Torday's relationship with Kikungulu, from whom he had literally wrestled free the unfortunate victim, was soured beyond repair. Kikungulu sought to poison Torday also; and when Torday sought to leave Kolokoto arrows were shot at him: 'At any rate', he wrote to Joyce, 'mark this: I collect the arrows for you' (24 July 1905).

This was savagery without nobility – the stuff of social evolution, unredeemed as yet by the strong streak of paternalism Torday later displayed. Indeed, Torday had already written to Joyce to say that though his 'pluck' might be misplaced he had come to the firm conclusion that the Mbala were what in a sense he had been encouraged to look for, 'a race on the lowest steps of civilisation' (16 July 1905). Material culture, he wrote, proved it: the Mbala had no poisoned arrows like the Bushmen, no canoes like Australian Aborigines, no harpoons and fish hooks like the people of Tierra del Fuego. All innovations in metallurgy, basketworking and animal husbandry were attributed to contact with neighbouring peoples. For ornaments they had only teeth, horns and bones, the raw materials of 'prehistoric man'. In art 'fetishes' were frequently carved, but as sculpture had no special power. It was the addition of *kisi*, a red clay inherited within families and embued with magical qualities, which was the important active agent. And 'in putting Kisi in a tree, it can serve as well as fetish as a wooden figure'. Though a challenging observation in terms of understanding the magical system of the Mbala and the place of figurative art within it, Torday at this stage of his anthropological career clearly meant the remark to be disparaging. As to language, it lacked the characteristics of sophisticated communication: 'not the slightest grammar can be found in it, it is a simple constellation of words'. Bows were the only unexpected element in this litany of the mental and material tool kit of the abjectly primitive. These were 'absolutely above their intelligence, showing real good work'. Someone, it seemed, must have taught the Mbala how to make them; it was clearly beyond their own abilities.

These private opinions did not make the printed page, of course; nor are they found in the factual reporting that characterises Torday's field-notes. In any case, Joyce tidied up all such subjective views to produce a more straightforward, neutral account of Mbala ethnography for publication. The only clearly pejorative material in the written accounts concerns cannibalism. Throughout the second half of the nineteenth century cannibalism was one of the few cultural characteristics consistently to attract comment in travellers' reports of Central Africa, especially those dealing with what is now northern Zaire. In the questionnaire the topic was neatly sandwiched between food and narcotics. Indeed, following that same format, in the report published in the joint names of both Torday

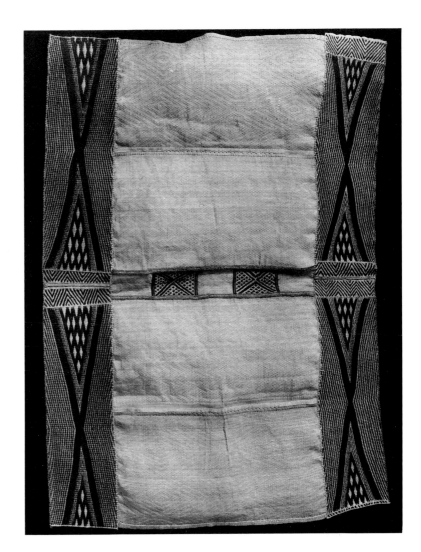

Raffia textile with pattern woven into the central panels and embroidered designs at the edges. The lozenge motif is thought to be derived from representations of the lizard. Mbuun. 1910.4–20.408. 103 × 71 cm. (This example was acquired – probably at Alela – in 1909 on a return trip Torday made to the Kwilu basin.)

and Joyce it comes under the heading of food, in a paragraph following one on domestic animals but before tobacco, snuff, hemp-smoking and drunkenness (1905, 404). And this is exactly how Torday was still presenting Mbala cannibalism in his popular account of 1913 – as a form of sustenance, if not an entirely wholesome one. Any conceptual basis for cannibalism was denied. Cannibals unashamedly liked human flesh and needed no further motivation.

There is, however, some distance between Torday's first impressions at Kolokoto and the caption to a photograph of an Mbala of the area in his later book: 'Although the traveller may at first be prejudiced against these people because of their well-known cannibalistic propensities, he will soon find out that they are very pleasant on the whole.' The note of quirky paternalism is tempered by a further unconventional touch in the next sentence: 'When kindly treated they are the most devoted servants one can imagine' (1913a, facing p. 86). During 1905 Torday had not yet reached this point of playful iconoclasm.

Arguably, the interest in cannibalism also served to deflect attention from other aspects of Mbala culture. Mbala accounts of origin talk of a period of unity under a single dominant ruler. This is a contrast with what is found in the present century when a chief like Kikungulu had a semi-independent status. Certain titles, however, are common throughout Mbala country. Of these Torday gave details of two, *muri* and *fumu*, though the exact distinction between them remains uncertain in his account. From later sources it seems that the main difference is between chiefs of the land (elsewhere called *muli* or *mudi*, Biebuyck 1985, 162) and chiefs of the village. Torday himself gives only a hint of this in the casual observation that among the more important privileges of *muri* are rights over parts of animals killed in the hunt, a feature which might in itself suggest a special ritual status in relation to the land. Failure to offer the requisite portion will result in future bad luck in hunting for those concerned. However, the main feature distinguishing *muri* in Torday and Joyce's estimation was the fact that apart from women they alone abstain from eating human flesh. This seemed remarkable 'especially when the primitive nature of their [Mbala generally] organisation is considered' (1905, 409). The presence or absence of cannibalism was so singular a litmus test of a society's state of advancement that finding both at once in the same social setting was unexpected. The further relations between ritual and political authority, the overlap between certain privileges of *muri* and *fumu*, and the implications of the prohibition on cannibalism among *muri* for the historical formation of Mbala society rest largely unexplored.

Muri also seem to have performed an important role in magical and medical practice, though again this is unclear. Torday talks of befriending a number of ritual specialists, among them Mwana N'Gombe, 'the great magician among the Ba-Mbala' (1905, 419). We are not told that he was necessarily *muri*. However, his three most important amulets are described as a bracelet (*mwena*), an axe, and a headcloth which was never removed and so embued with magical power that he could not look at it, even in a mirror, for fear he would die. Elsewhere we gather that the wearing of a special headcloth and possession of *mwena*, which could only be inherited, never bought, were distinctive of *muri*. The implication that *muri* were ritual specialists can be deduced from the text, but it is not made apparent. The technique of working through the questionnaire did not in the end encourage a questioning attitude; it tended to lead to the descriptive listing of features but frustrated pursuing broader questions across categories.

Torday collected examples of the *muri* iron bracelet and the raffia headcloth, both of which he regarded as significant acquisitions. They are, however, replicas, as they must be since the supporting ethnography indicates that separation from inherited, original examples of such regalia would alienate a *muri* and his descendants from their social class. Such objects, even though they may appear to the untutored unprepossessing in character, are important sources of legitimacy. Torday was sufficiently sensitive to the implications of this to avoid any more interventionist method of collection. This also applied to other categories of ritually important object he acquired among the northern groups of Mbala. There are, for instance, six figures in the collection, five from Kolokoto and one from Mokunji, a village to the south. Such figures are consulted by ritual specialists either singly, or in male and female pairs, on behalf of clients. They are interrogated on such subjects as the cause of ill fortune, or the most advisable course of future action, and respond through the medium of the diviner who speaks out when in a state of trance. It is the *kisi*, the red clay applied to the object, which is identified as the source of their familiar's ability to enter trance and solve problems. We have no details of the circumstances of their collection, but it is noticeable that only one of the figures appears to have been recently used at the time of acquisition on the evidence of the surface accumulation of red powder. The others, though apparently made to act as a vehicle of *kisi*, have been collected unused.

Chokwe elephant hunter. A painting by Norman Hardy executed after a photograph taken in the Kwilu by Torday and Hilton-Simpson in 1909.

The Yaka

From Kolokoto Torday travelled south, again with his Mbala retinue for company and with no direct contact with Europeans. It was November 1905 before he returned to the Kwilu River with its boat connections to the Kasai and its network of trading stations. Torday makes little mention in any of the accounts, including his letters to Joyce, of what he was doing on these trips beyond his ethnographic work. That he was trading on behalf of the Kasai Company is apparent only in the precise nature of the reports he provides on local systems of marketing, economic interchange, and the varieties of local currencies and their relative values. And the collection of indigenous forms of currency Torday made is especially well documented. The most widespread medium of exchange was a shell known locally as *djimbu* (identified as *Olivella nana*), reputedly introduced by the Portuguese as a medium of trade. This could also be transferred at recognised rates of exchange into one of several other currencies – salt, hoe blades, or one of several standard types of iron product, whether in the form of retangular blocks or iron plates, all made from locally smelted iron.

Much of this second half of the year Torday was still in Mbala country. He did, however, venture into adjacent parts of Yaka territory. He began work among the Yaka mainly through the medium of the Mbala language, which was also understood by many native Yaka-speakers. By collecting Yaka vocabularies through a related Bantu tongue he declared himself well able to follow conversations after only a short time; in due course he was able to speak Yaka fluently. More than that, however, the characteristics of Mbala life were becoming a yardstick by which to assess other peoples of the Kwilu area, predictably enough for information was being gathered on essentially similar themes. The published account of Yaka ethnography (Torday and Joyce 1906a) even included a table listing all the points of difference between the Yaka and Mbala as revealed by the completed questionnaires.

The features enumerated are as unrelated to each other as those on any randomly prepared list. They include the presence (Yaka) and absence (Mbala) of circumcision, of tattooing, an insistence or otherwise on the virginity of brides, the treatment of slaves, drunks and cripples (the Mbala being more respectful of slaves, the Yaka more tolerant of the other two), and the Yaka abhorrence of cannibalism by contrast with the Mbala taste for it (Torday and Joyce 1906a, 41). It would be hard to find any systematic social or historical links that might explain those elements that are in the list, or indeed those that are not. The table of features hardly constitutes more than the barest preliminary to a comparative sociology.

At one level a lingering belief that tribal life could be characterised as a kind of closed cell could cope well enough with this lack of fit even between two neighbouring societies. The relatively separate and pristine condition of peoples remote from the great spurs to development arising from contact with 'civilised' levels of culture had been taken for granted. As it happens, Torday was already collecting a considerable body of evidence which might seem to suggest the exact opposite. The Kwilu Basin, according to all the historical accounts he was accumulating, had been

Wood charm in the form of a
blacksmith's bellows with a leather
thong strung with blue glass beads.
Worn by members of the chiefly clan,
Kwese. 1907.5–28.307.
L. (including thong) 19.5 cm.

occupied relatively recently and had been the scene of an immense amount
of intermingling and cultural interchange. After all, almost every Mbala
art, in Torday's description, is attributed an exotic origin. The Yaka had
instituted certain rules conducive to 'national purity'; they had avoided
intermingling and appeared self-reliant, except in so far as a knowledge
of metallurgy was concerned, this having been learnt from the Mbala (who
are themselves characterised as having learnt it elsewhere). But in the
course of expansion they had necessarily had the problem of what to do
about conquered peoples. The answer, Torday tells us, had in large
measure been enslavement (Torday and Joyce 1906a, 40). The Yaka did
not intermarry extensively with the vanquished; their society was thus
a tiered one composed of a variety of social classes of differing ethnic background. The obvious characterisation which emerges from Torday's information is of Yaka society as a satellite of Kwilu cultures sheltering beneath
the umbrella of an ideal of the purity of Yaka ethnicity. Even in the case
of so independent a people as the Yaka, the unique cultural 'cell' turns
out to be somewhat more molecular than might have been anticipated
on the basis of at least one strain of evolutionist thought.

Torday's ethnography, however, was not forged in the heat of evolutionist debate, nor the results assessed in the light of such considerations.
Neither he nor Joyce, to judge by the published articles, was concerned
with theoretical implications; they present the ethnographic report in the
spirit of descriptive science. In effect, what they were concerned with in
this early phase of their co-operation was typologies: people constituted
not as individuals but as representatives of some greater cultural entity,
and societies portrayed not as dynamic structures but as reified skeletal
constructs of social practice. 'Though the Ba-Yaka are in close touch with
the Ba-Mbala, they seem to resemble them but slightly except in so far
as the culture of both tribes is of the primitive West African type' (Torday
and Joyce 1906a, 40). Charting the variations within a given cultural
typology was the primary aim.

The second feature of Torday's investigations in the less accessible areas
of the Kwilu is his increasing level of engagement with the peoples amongst
whom he was working. Bushcraft was one of Torday's favourite subjects,
and in his own autobiographical reflections we rarely see him make mis-
takes, still less made a fool of. 'The *ideal* traveller', he wrote, 'has no adven-
tures; for if the white man gets into a scrape it is generally his own fault
and not that of the native' (1913, 18). Being poisoned by your hosts is
something that happens to other people, and to Torday only at the start
of his work, not when he was more confident and involved.

Thus, for instance, in the district of Zange two important Yaka masks,
Kikunga and Hemba, were kept together in a single hut. Torday, as a condition of being able to see them, agreed to make a suitable prestation through
their custodian. The former mask was described (1913a, 151) as excep-
tionally large, over one metre in height, and was presumably of the *kakungu*
type, the enormous male masks often identified with the Suku but here
also located for the first time among the Yaka (a provenance later confirmed by Plancquert 1930; see also Biebuyck 1985, 182, and Bourgeois

1980). The Hemba mask is identified by Torday as smaller, an 'ordinary mask' (151). The type is again shared with the Suku and is a helmet mask usually surmounted by a figure or a bird. Torday collected one such mask with a monkey-like animal on the crest in Zange. Whether it is the same one seen on the occasion described is unclear.

The main implication of working with and through local forms of politesse, however, had been well learnt. Torday later returned to the event as part of the bush wisdom he felt himself uniquely placed to pass on to the less experienced: 'A small present to the village fetish is often of greater

Wood mask with black raffia fringe. Yaka. 1907.5–28.155. H. 36 cm. (Collected at Zange.)

use than a big present given to the chief. I have read somewhere of a man who gained a great reputation for amiability by the simple device of offending everyone in order to have an opportunity of offering a humble apology; this may seem very funny, but in practice it works exceedingly well' (1913a, 235).

Peoples of the Upper Kwilu

During 1906 Torday had two principal bases. The first was at Luano, a settlement established only a decade earlier and lying on the Kwilu between Dima and Kongo; the villages of the region were mainly occupied by (northern) Mbala, Yansi and Hungaan. His second base, from the middle of the year onwards, was further downriver at Kikwit, where he had the opportunity to study both the peoples he came to designate as southern Mbala and neighbouring peoples such as the Mbuun.

As always the starting-point of research was the questionnaire, now recommended directly in one of the written reports (1906b, 275) as an appropriate framework within which data could be collected and structured. Again, too, the checklist of features was applied cross-culturally, the Hungaan, for example, being compared to the Teke (from whom

Southern Bambala Gamblers.

'Southern Bambala (i.e. Mbala) gamblers'.

Torday and Joyce suggest, probably erroneously, the Hungaan derive) and to the Mbala (272–4). The aim remained essentially descriptive; yet there is evident the beginnings of a broader disquiet with the practice of drawing comparisons, not perhaps between adjacent populations but between African and European 'civilisation' generally. '. . . it is ridiculous', wrote Torday and Joyce, 'to clothe a primitive people in a civilisation made to the measure of someone else and expect the result to be a good fit. Human nature is plastic, but not so fluid as to take the form of any mould into which it is poured' (274–5). The Hungaan lack of familiarity with mathematical calculation, for instance, does not derive from a lack of intelligence, any more than does a European inability to identify details of the natural environment or the precise direction of a sudden noise. 'Judged by such a test, the native is as superior to the European as the latter to the former in mental arithmetic' (277).

The collections made by Torday to an extent reflect this emphasis on the more practical aspects of both Hungaan and Yansi cognition and on technological features of their culture. It ranges from such severely utilitarian items as instruments for the castration of animals or representative armouries of weapons from all the peoples visited to a large series of basketry types deliberately collected to demonstrate varieties of form and

Wood figure with a fibre coiffure and the surface reddened through repeated application of *kisi* to empower it magically. Southern Mbala. 1907.5–28.107. H. 58 cm. (Collected at Kikwit.)

techniques of manufacture. Parts of the latter series were published (Torday and Joyce 1906b, pls XXXIII and IV) together with a detailed technical description. Similarly, a special catalogue, which remained unpublished and is now unfortunately missing, was produced identifying the variations of pattern in a collection of sixty-three raffia cloths from the Yansi and Mbala. Joyce himself published a separate study of Mbuun weaving at a later stage concentrating again largely on technological features (1925).

To the modern student of the arts of the Kwilu, however, it is the sculpture of the Mbala, and especially of the southern groups, which constitutes perhaps the most familiar and distinctive set of images of all (see, for example, Biebuyck 1985, pls 29–36). Some 200 examples are known (Bourgeois 1988, 13), including complex maternity figures and musicians. Among their distinguishing features is a high-ridged style of coiffure, which Torday's field photographs and written descriptions show to have also been current in the opening decade of the century, and sharply filed teeth, an aspect of Mbala culture not found among either the Hungaan or Yansi. Such objects appear to have formed part of royal treasures and to have been associated with the exercise of various kinds of mystical power (Biebuyck 1985, 161–71). Interestingly, Torday collected no figures in this style. Indeed, only one piece even shows the coiffure that is so readily identified as a marker of southern Mbala ethnicity, and that is a small figurative charm worn round the neck by southern Mbala men. There are more figures in the collection formed among the northern Mbala which show southern styles of coiffure than are found among the material Torday acquired in his various sorties from Kikwit.

It is tempting to suggest that this is in part because Torday's essentially documentary intentions led him, as he assured Hercules Read they did, to value anthropological interests above aesthetics, and he did not therefore necessarily seek out 'art' objects as a priority for the collection. There is something to be said for this, though it should be added that it was not until the 1920s (and possibly as much as two decades after Torday's departure) that larger figures in what is now seen as the Mbala style were produced in the Kikwit area (Bourgeois 1988, 22–3). And Torday also felt that one such figure later illustrated in von Sydow was not in fact Mbala at all, his evidence being again that of coiffure (1931e, 244). Of two large figures acquired by Torday from the southern Mbala one is a snuff mortar from the River Yambesi and the other, from Kikwit itself, is described as a vehicle (or 'idol') for *kisi*. The emphasis in the documentation, in other words, is on how and where the sculpture fits into a society's activities, whether domestic or magical. The point emerges even more strongly in the notes accompanying the Hungaan collection. A wood figure topped with long horns is described as 'a fancy carving', whilst the very next object in the collection is 'a box containing the *real* Bahuana [i.e. Hungaan] fetishes' (my emphasis) – the fetishes consisting of a number of cloth bundles and animal remains. The southern Mbala collection too contains a series of naturally occurring substances, variously wrapped in hide and cloth packets, that are used in magical contexts. The anthropological importance of these visually unprepossessing items rendered them on a level with the more aesthetically interesting objects to which some of them were applied.

'Anthropological importance' was at least partly a matter of establishing the function of an object. More importantly, however, it was also a question of recording all the clues, no matter how humble they might initially appear, that could be relevant to the essential task Torday and Joyce were increasingly to regard as one proper to anthropology, that of historical reconstruction. Writing excitedly to Joyce from Luano in early 1906, Torday had said 'we shall try and put some order in our ideas and then publish our famous paper "On movements of some Bantu races" or "The Central African Völkerwanderung" at the Royal Society, astonish the scientific world, be made honorary members of innumerable British and foreign scientific societies – just like Mr. Pickwick' (29 January). History was to be, as in the Old Testament, a history of wandering tribes, with an emphasis on the order of arrival of peoples in a region.

The imagined paper was eventually published, though with little fanfare and under a less dramatic title – 'On the Ethnology of the South-Western Congo Free State' (Torday and Joyce 1907b). The careful listing and comparison of cultural features had allowed the oddities of Kwilu culture to be identified and common traits assimilated to existing typologies. In the collection of ethnographical objects, for instance, the incongruities of Kwese coiled basketry, or Mbuun wood swords, when compared with other techniques of manufacture and object types in the area, were suggestive. Consideration of a wide range of such features could, it was thought, help establish the antiquity of certain peoples in a region, the level of contact that had taken place between them and other historical communities, and the general direction of the migration which they had followed to establish themselves in their present home. Behind the plea to researchers to avoid ill-considered comparisons between African and European civilisation in general lay an emerging preference for local histories deduced from ethnographical evidence rather than from grandiose schemes of human evolution.

Ethnography and the administration of the Congo State

This article reviewing the whole two years' work in the Kwilu also had another interesting feature: it starts with an attack on the veracity of the information collected and then beginning to be published by the German explorer Leo Frobenius, and it ends with a tribute by Joyce, appended under his own name, to the methods pursued by Torday and the reliance that can be placed in information gathered by someone with mastery of four Kwilu languages.

Torday himself felt that during his residence in Kikwit he had established a kinship with the southern Mbala which allowed him not only to record their culture but, in a sense, to act as a spokesman for it. He had become a significant member of Mbala society in his own right. His native name was Deke (derived from his earlier experience in the south-east of the Congo State where he was known by the Swahili term for a bird). So many chil-

Wood cup. Generally cups in this style simply employ lozenge motifs, as on Mbuun textiles. Here, however, the whole cup has been reconceived as a female figure. Mbuun. 1910.4–20.186. H. 12 cm. (Collected, probably from the village of Alela, in 1909.)

The riverbank at Kikwit on the Kwilu.

dren were named after him in his time in Kikwit that Torday foresaw the risk of some future ill-informed ethnographer (we know from his letters that he had Frobenius in mind) would come to designate the people of the area as the Badeke. According to Torday's own somewhat romanticised account (1913a, 267–8), there was not a dry eye to be found in Kikwit when, early in 1907, the moment came for him to leave. Delegations arrived from surrounding chiefs imploring him to stay, asking what they had done to cause his departure. Hundreds of hands had to be shaken in leave-taking and the heads of the many baby Dekes patted; and with the boat being pushed from the jetty the assembled citizenry broke into Torday's favourite song.

Much of Torday's later reflection on this period of his life took the form of an account of the many lessons he had learnt in his two years as a trader-cum-ethnographer. Such worldly advice was issued as more than a series of incidental hints for travellers. For one thing, practical know-how also had practical administrative applications. Just as field-based anthropology was in its infancy, so too government anthropologists were yet to become an established feature of the colonial enterprise. When in

1926 Evans-Pritchard first visited the Azande in the south-western corner of the Sudan, it was with the support, both moral and financial, of the Anglo-Egyptian Government. The Provincial Governor of the area was himself a scholar-administrator, Major P.M. Larken. Larken, Evans-Pritchard wrote, 'regarded my work as something from which the Azande might derive benefit and that justified it in his opinion' (Evans-Pritchard 1937, viii). For Torday, when recalling his own experience, the issue seemed not so much one of providing knowledge of indigenous custom to promote better administration as something much more basic and more urgent – that of telling administrators and agents of trading companies how to behave. Reminiscence provided an idiosyncratic way of laying down what he came to see as guidelines for good government – never strike 'a native' (1913a, 185), keep your temper and never scold a man (191), always show 'respect towards objects or acts connected with the native ideas of religion' (235), never say anything that might even seem untrue and never boast (236), and remember you are an intruder for 'colonisation itself is an injustice' (243).

This advice was written down in reflection well after the event. However, for Torday in the field in 1905–6 – confident, linguistically able and impatient of the self-righteous – maladministration and misunderstanding on the part of the authorities were issues to be exposed and resolved. 'The greatest obstacle to the administration of justice', he wrote, 'is the solidarity of the Europeans and the natural reluctance of everyone to report to a magistrate the misdeeds of a fellow white man' (1913a, 247). In his own right the 'English spy' was instrumental in bringing a number of Europeans before the judicial authorities of the Congo State, taking the side of what he often saw as the luckless recipients of external government before intrusive and ill-informed officialdom.

Similarly, Torday was never reluctant to forestall official intervention by himself seeking to sort out conflicts before they came under the scrutiny of the administration. Thus when he first arrived at Luano he quickly set about resolving an armed conflict that had been running between the Yansi and an alliance of Mbala and Ngongo. His method was to start by negotiating with both sides separately and in their own territory. Going directly to Chitutu, an important Yansi chief, he immediately deferred to local practice in making his customary gift to the chiefly fetishes. Sitting down, he tells us (1913a, 164–5), he resorted to a 'sovereign remedy' when confronted by suspicion: he took out a copy of the *Graphic* magazine and turned to the page with an advertisement for Monkey Brand Soap. The curious onlookers were greatly amused by the image; confidence in the motives of this unconventional outsider began to grow, and from a position of trust Torday was in due course able to conclude a treaty between the contending parties.

Playfulness came naturally to Torday, but the idea of carrying illustrations as part of his baggage was not, he readily admitted, one of his own. He had originally been advised to do so by the eminent British administrator Sir H.H. Johnston, one of the most powerful voices enlisted by the Congo Reform Association in mounting its critique of Leopold's distant colony.

Wood charm in a style already regarded as obsolete when Torday collected this example. Southern Mbala. 1907.5–28.82. H. 10 cm.

To Johnston, as to Torday, sympathetic engagement of the kind implied by anthropological work seemed a prerequisite of sensitive government; but in Torday's case there was sometimes an unexpected edge to such sentiment. Where benign administration was often lacking, the anthropologist could emerge as more than simply an apologist for local custom. 'The whole country', Torday wrote from Luano, 'recognises me as its great chief and if I wanted to establish a little monarchy here I could resist State forces for a considerable time. This is so far recognised by the authorities that if natives do some mischief and have to be arrested, they simply informe [*sic*] me and I just let the local chief know whom I want and he (the man I want) is brought to me and given up, without murmur.' Torday may have concluded his letter on a note of embarrassment – 'There', he wrote, 'you [Joyce] have got an egotistical letter; don't be angry, I won't do it again' (25 May 1906) – but it is not difficult to see how he came to have a reputation with his employers as being at the same time peacemaker and trouble-maker.

Torday and Frobenius

Beyond its political implications Torday also offered up his reflections as an object lesson in ethnographic technique. The message was the same one as that intended for the administrator. For one thing humour played a significant part in Torday's approach in the field – the phonograph he used to record native music was also used to give concerts in the field, 'laughing songs' being a particular favourite. Torday never made fun of indigenous custom, and was never censorious, but equally he was far from being unrelentingly stuffy and high-minded. Indeed, he regarded an ability to translate humour as a hallmark of gifted fieldwork. A capacity for amiability was for Torday as important a prerequisite of successful fieldwork as any more technical ethnographic instruction. He was not providing an introduction to details of method; his interest was in giving an impression of the quality of relationship that ethnographic research implied. This was more than homespun philosophising; it was an expression of the belief, already confirmed when Torday came to write his biographical account, that authentic ethnography begins with qualitative experience. To know a culture is not only to be able to record its leading features, it is also to know how to live and work within it.

Frobenius was the counterpoint to everything Torday had to say. The two had met in the Congo early in 1905 over an improbable tea of gin and various 'dainty cakes' prepared by Torday himself. Torday later recalled the event, with Frobenius thinly disguised as an exceedingly Teutonic 'martial gentleman', 'as fully armed as Tweedledum and Tweedledee' (1913a, 75). Frobenius was travelling with a companion, the painter Hans-Frederick Lemme. They got off on quite the wrong foot with Torday, first by alarming the villagers round his settlement by arriving with revolvers and rifles ostentatiously displayed, and secondly by benefacting upon Torday himself their own version of bushcraft in the mistaken belief that he was new to the Tropics. However, the need to conceal, albeit with deliberate imperfection, Frobenius' identity came from the discreditable comments Torday passed on Frobenius' behaviour in the pursuit of science. The unpublished remarks are still more of a seering indictment than the published. 'If you know', Torday wrote to Joyce, 'how Frobenius proceeded to obtain notes about the natives, you would not even read anything he may write. He is a German and has proceeded as a German; not with Germanic thoroughness, but in giving orders to his interpreter to obtain information; and as the fellow knew he would be thrashed if he got none he always obtained some, or at least pretended to have got it from the natives' (2 June 1906). The colonial administrator Charles Partridge had similar things to say about a separate visit Frobenius made to Nigeria. This was not forsaking the armchair for the field; this was transporting it fully sprung into the 'Heart of Darkness' and exulting in its comforts.

Torday's whole nature was in revolt against such behaviour, whether in the name of science or not. His temperamental preference was that of personal engagement. He was quite prepared to negotiate between warring villages or rescue unwitting victims of witchcraft from being buried alive; but to do either effectively required an intimate knowledge of indigenous language and culture. Torday was a champion of direct solid experience: to that extent ethnography was for him an extension of bushcraft.

The distinction between Torday's approach and that of Frobenius is neatly summed up in the contrast between the published illustrations of

Torday doing fieldwork among the
Kuba-Ngongo.

each of them doing fieldwork in the Congo State. The Torday photograph
(published in Hilton-Simpson 1911, 105) is on an intimate scale. He is
seen sideways on – the camera, as it were, is looking over his shoulder.
The centre of the photo and of attention is the person with whom Torday
is talking, a frail elderly man identified as the 'Bilumbu' of the Kuba. A
younger woman and man sit behind and a child at the side. The palm-fibre
wall at the back of the photograph confirms that the picture was taken
in a Kuba enclosure. Torday is leaning forward attentively. The atmo-
sphere is informal but intense.

   The Frobenius illustration by contrast is a painting (1907, opp. 424).
Frobenius is shown by candlelight beneath the awning of his tent, seated,
notebook and pen in hand. It is he who is the focus of the illustration,
not his 'informants'. Frobenius' companion, the painter Hans-Frederick
Lemme, is shown playing the lute. At the fringes of the picture, in the
gloom, sit the informants shown for the most part from the back (and
thus occupying the same general position as Torday does in the photograph of him in the field). The painting, though obviously done after the
event and thus capable of manipulation to present the participants in what

Frobenius doing fieldwork in the Congo. After a painting reproduced in Frobenius 1907, pl. XXXI, opposite p. 424.

would be considered the best light, shows a style of fieldwork which is more formal and distant, lacking the friendly intimacy of the Torday photograph. The informants have come to see Frobenius; they are in his territory on his terms. They have not come to discuss but to give up secrets.

The distinction is an interesting one. In the Torday photograph the emphasis is less on Torday and more on the quality of a particular relationship which he is engaged in creating. The Frobenius picture, by contrast, gives a somewhat bucolic impression; the emphasis is on a certain quality of life enjoyed by 'the explorer'. The informants are presented as if they are the audience and Frobenius the principal actor, rather than the other way round. He is in the light, and enlightened; they are in semi-obscurity.

Where Frobenius served up facts as fodder for the theorist, Torday had begun to anticipate the development of a whole tradition of fieldwork in British anthropology where firsthand insight counted above bare facts vacuum-packed for transport back to the university study. The Torday photograph, however, derives from 1908 and his final expedition to Central Africa. By then the set of apparently objective controls represented by the questionnaire and the camera were ceasing to be ends in themselves.

4 Into the 'Kingdom of Shamba the Great'

Torday returned to England on 16 March 1907. What he would do next was unclear, though it seemed certain he would again have to go abroad. 'I am afraid that when I shall be able to settle in Europe', he had written before leaving the Congo, 'I shall be an old fellow, with a bad liver and a bad temper and at last shall marry my cook, to have someone to make my gruel. Fine prospects!' (2 June 1906). He did not necessarily seek a return passage to Central Africa; indeed, involvement in some, probably British, colonial enterprise seemed the likeliest course; he was contemplating taking the relevant examinations to qualify him for such a posting.

The final parts of his 1905-7 collection, however, already included a disparate range of objects from peoples such as the Kuba, Lele, Kete, Songo Meno and Tetela – peoples living in the Kasai and Sankuru Basins to the east of the Kwilu. It is very unlikely that Torday acquired the items himself in the field; they may well have come to him through his contacts in the Kasai Company from whom, also, it is probable he acquired a photograph of the Kuba king which he was later able to present to him. The collection, small as it was, confirmed the impression of earlier travellers – especially Dr Wolf, a member of the Wissmann expedition, who had skirted the area in 1884, or the Black American missionary William Shepherd who was the first to penetrate the Kuba kingdom itself – that this was indeed a region of considerable interest. Just six months later, on 1 October 1907, Torday was again embarked for the mouth of the Congo committed to two years' exploration of what promised to be a significant cultural and artistic centre.

Previously, of course, Torday had always managed to combine field enthnography with some other form of gainful employment. The British Museum authorities, in consultation with whom the whole expedition was planned, were Torday's official sponsors; that, however, did not mean that they were able to act as his exclusive financial backers. Equally, the Royal Society when approached was unwilling to support a Hungarian citizen even if attached to a British institution. The news was communicated to Torday when he was already back in the field and working with his British colleague, M.W. Hilton-Simpson. Torday's response in a letter to Joyce was typically robust: 'My complements [sic] to the Royal Society and many thanks. Of course they are quite right, as Hilton-Simpson is an undesirable alien, just as I am, and as we collect exclusively for alien museums and our information shall be all published in Chinese in Tierra del Fuego' (15 May 1908). For its part, the Council of the Royal Anthropological Institute replied that its role was to promote publications, not field research. Ironically, Torday was later to receive the Institute's Rivers Medal (named after W.H.R. Rivers) in recognition of the quality of his fieldwork, as in due course did Hilton-Simpson for subsequent fieldwork undertaken in North Africa. There was one more procedure he might have followed to obtain financial support: that adopted by Frobenius who in large measure financed his explorations from profits made on the sale of the artefacts he brought back. But Torday was as reluctant to follow Frobenius in this strategy as he was in everything else.

At the outset Torday had anticipated being able to recover his costs by

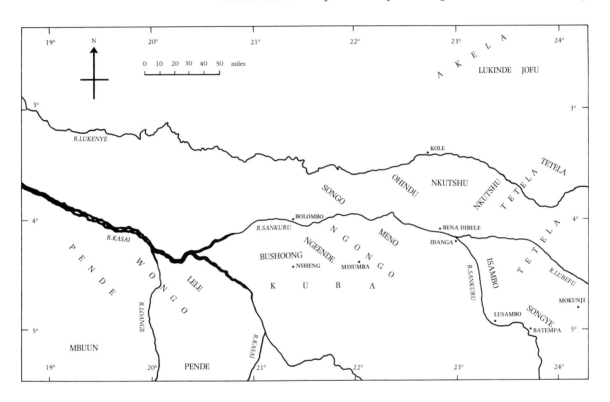

The Kasai and Sankuru basins.

writing a popular account of his travels on his return. In the event, however, funds became short well before that. He contemplated clearing debts incurred with the Kasai Company by offering them his part of any copyright fees he might subsequently receive from translations of the published ethnography of the Kasai region. In the end he was obliged to write in apologetic vein to Hercules Read asking if the British Museum could reimburse him to whatever level it was able and saw fit for the objects he was sending back (which by then – August 1908 – already numbered forty-eight large crates). The actual cost, he explained, was more than the Museum might find reasonable, especially if it were obliged to include the costs incurred in porterage, freighting and documentation. In addition some items were obtained at a cost so beyond what the Museum authorities might anticipate that he felt he must bear the bulk of it himself – 'for example like Bankutu currency worth five slaves!' Personal gain was never

The Kuba king, Kot aPe, painted by
Norman Hardy from a photograph.

one of Torday's motivations, but although he still had an income from
his family estates in Hungary, he lacked the private resources to make
completely magnanimous donations.

These considerations also help explain another feature of Torday's
1907–9 work – the fact that it was undertaken in the context of an 'expedition'. Until then he had always conducted his research alone. Indeed, in
Africa he was often irritated by the society of Europeans, and at no point
in either his letters or his pubished writing did he ever complain of long
periods of isolation in the company of Congolese. This was not forbearance;
he preferred it that way, much that he regretted the effects it was having
on his prospects of finding a suitable bride. When recalling those Europeans
he had met who attracted him most (1925a, 31), he characteristically
came up not with that rare enough phenomenon at the time, a sympathetic
administrator, or a missionary, but with 'Dirty Jim' – an Englishman who
had deliberately lost himself in the Forests, avoided recognised routes and
dealt exclusively with Africans on some mysterious business of his own.
Torday once persuaded the residents of an isolated mission station to invite
'Dirty Jim' to afternoon tea and – more difficult – persuaded Dirty Jim to
come too, principally it seems on the promise that he would thereby be
able to see a European woman again. The pleasant, elderly wife of the
missionary could not get Jim to speak. Furthermore, he broke down and
wept on discovering he had been given a bag of doughnuts as a leaving
present. Torday certainly had not gone bush to this extent, but he readily
endorsed the self-contained competence of those able to enjoy long periods
of simplicity and isolation in Africa. His model was David Livingstone.

An 'expedition', albeit on a small scale, was, therefore, a new departure
for Torday, and not one he might have been expected to welcome
unreservedly. Furthermore, it was not that, as Haddon had done in preparing his Torres Straits research, members were recruited because they had
special skills or could undertake particular responsibilities. The only exception was the inclusion for the first six months of Norman Hardy, a recognised painter who had travelled extensively in the South Pacific and
developed a preference for ethnographic subjects; and Torday had to meet
the expense of Hardy's journey from his own limited resources.

M.W. Hilton-Simpson joined Torday at Joyce's suggestion, when he himself was unable to participate as he had originally planned. Hilton-Simpson
had already undertaken three years' exploration of the Barbary States and
had been on the point of mounting his own expedition to the Sahara. In
the summer of 1907, however, difficulties between France and Morocco
led to independent travel through the area being curtailed. Hilton-Simpson
had neither experience of Central Africa nor, as yet, a grounding in ethnography other than that acquired by someone with experience of passing
time in remote places. He was essentially a traveller and keen sportsman
in the mould of the Powell-Cotton family, with whom he had links; he
was an 'all-rounder', a Fellow at once of the Royal Geographical Society,
the Zoological Society and the Royal Anthropological Institute. Hilton-
Simpson did, however, have resources that could immediately be transferred to Torday's venture. He also brought with him his travelling

Torday preparing to make a phonograph recording of Songye musicians.

companion enlisted for the Saharan crossing, together with the necessary subscription that went with inclusion in the expedition. Though the person recruited, Iredell, disembarked and took a boat home as soon as they reached the Congo estuary, he did at least leave behind over half of the contribution he had made to expedition funds. Further assistance came from C.G. Seligman who provided photographic equipment, and from Henry Wellcome whose pharmaceutical firm, Burroughs and Wellcome, gave Torday a large supply of suitable drugs in return for the promise of a selection of objects for his ethnographical collection. Torday could not have sustained two years' uninterrupted fieldwork without such financial and practical support; even so, he was for ever teetering on the brink of falling into deficit with his bankers in the Congo, the Liverpool-based trading company of Hatton and Cookson and the Kasai Company.

Despite Torday's impatience of some Europeans he had met in Central Africa, relations between him, Hilton-Simpson and Hardy were on the whole good. In the published acknowledgements each is given due credit for their part in securing the positive results of the expedition. Hilton-Simpson further commended Torday's pleasant companionship in his own account of their travels, adding that their two years had passed without the semblance of a dispute (1911, xiii). Privately each also commented favourably on the other's qualities – Hilton-Simpson was described by Torday as 'a brick' (11 October 1907), whilst Hilton-Simpson remarked 'personally I find T very easy to get on with and the way he has run this show so far has been splendid' (6 April 1908). Hilton-Simpson readily took on the task of keeping a detailed diary of events (subsequently deposited in the Royal Anthropological Institute) and of making all the zoological observations, in part as an adjunct to his hunting activities. He discovered, for example, a new type of buffalo subsequently named after him: *Bos caffer simpsoni*. It is also likely he took the majority of the photographs resulting from the expedition. He became, Torday recorded, 'simply invaluable' (1910a, 53).

Hardy for his part made a large number of sketches which were worked up later as paintings and he also worked from photographs provided by Torday and Hilton-Simpson covering those areas that he did not himself visit. His early departure, however, was not a matter of great regret to the other two, whatever the picture of general harmony subsequently reported. He had not taken well to the rigours of travel in the Congo State, refusing for instance to travel anywhere by dug-out canoe. 'I don't think', Hilton-Simpson wrote, 'he [Hardy] quite approves of the existence of Africa' (6 April 1908); or again, in Torday's comments on his failure to keep in touch after his departure, 'Artist or no artist he might possess some rudimentary knowledge of manners' (12 October 1908).

The itinerary

The starting-point of the expedition was, as it had been in 1905, at Dima, a European settlement situated on the Kasai River itself just above the mouth of the Kwango. Dima's development as a trading centre, and as the headquarters of the Kasai Company, derived from its location at the confluence of these river systems. A short stay here was necessary to await the arrival of supplies from the coast. By early December 1907 the expedition was ready to travel up the Kasai and Sankuru Rivers as far as Batempa, which was finally reached on Christmas Eve. The ultimate destination was Mokunji, an overland trek to the Lubefu River. About six weeks were spent here before returning to the Sankuru and travelling back from Batempa to Lusambo, by then a large town of some 40,000 inhabitants, where they arrived at the end of February 1908.

Only a few weeks were spent at Lusambo, so that by mid-March all three had travelled back upriver as far as Gandu, from which they were able to walk to Misumba. The next month was largely spent here, though Torday also visited the western side of the Lubudi River several days distant. The fruitfulness of their work in and around Misumba, amongst eastern sections of the Kuba, persuaded them that it would be best to try and visit the capital itself, something which had not been envisaged at the outset. It was, however, already mid-April. Hardy's period with the expedition was virtually at an end. Better, therefore, to return to Gandu to see Hardy off and then travel to the north of the Sankuru completing that part of the projected work before returning to the Kuba.

Thus, after Hardy's departure Torday and Hilton-Simpson returned downriver again as far as Bena Dibele, a small Government post, where they set about planning a visit into what was then Leopold's *domain privé*. Apart from occasional Government officials they were the first Europeans to investigate these areas within the orbit of the Equatorial Forest proper. The first aim was to reach Kole on the Lukenye River and thence to go along the river as far as Lodja from which a trip still further to the north could be undertaken. This was to occupy them from May until August when they marched back to the Sankuru at Idanga, the point of its confluence with the Lubefu.

By the end of the first week of September the two had travelled upstream again to Bolombo, the nearest point on the Sankuru from which the Kuba capital at Nsheng could be reached (and the place at which Frobenius had acquired the bulk of his Kuba collection several years earlier). Although it was barely sixteen years since the first foreigner, William Sheppard, had visited the king, there were already quite a number of Europeans who had followed in his wake. On the Sankuru Torday and Hilton-Simpson had met the British Consul, Captain Thesiger, who had recently been at Nsheng; and on arrival at the capital itself they were met by the king in company with a Belgian priest (a Catholic mission had been established as early as 1904). Even so, Torday was the first ethnographer to visit the king, and they remained in close contact throughout their stay which lasted until just before Christmas 1908.

Nsheng at the time of their visit was still suffering from the effects of an uprising some four years previously and was poorly supplied with livestock. Torday's own resources were also coming to an end. With a diet increasingly reliant on what Hilton-Simpson could provide with his rifle (which meant that the meat had often gone rotten by the time it reached Torday) both had suffered bouts of illness. They thus spent the latter part of January and early February recuperating at Dima and at the Jesuit mission at Pana on the Kwilu, before going on to Kikwit where Torday had taken his tearful farewells nearly two years previously.

Kikwit was reached on 21 February 1909, and the next three months were spent travelling southwards following the course of the Kwilu and then across country to the banks of the River Loange. In letters Torday talked of the Loange as their Rubicon. The land lying between it and the Kasai had never been traversed. Filling in this blank on the map had been one of the declared aims of the expedition. It was said to be dangerous country. Torday and Hilton-Simpson opted to cross it, as was their practice, without armed escort. The journey lasted two months, and when in late July they arrived on the banks of the Kasai rumours of their demise at the hands of the inhabitants of the region had already reached the ears of the British Consul in Boma. But by September 1909 their journeying had come to an end, and they had returned to England to prove that the rumours were indeed exaggerated. 'Dear So-and-so,' someone had written to a friend in the British Museum, 'I am just back from the Congo. I suppose you have heard that Torday and his companion have been killed and eaten by the Bashilele? I hope you are quite well' (Torday 1925a, 74).

Songye musicians and dancers.

Recounting the itinerary of the expedition in this way gives a good indication of the work on which Torday and Hilton-Simpson were engaged. In 1913 W.H.R. Rivers outlined the kind of fieldwork towards which all the significant developments of the opening decade of the century seemed to point. 'A typical piece of intensive work', Rivers wrote, 'is one in which the worker lives for a year or more among a community of perhaps four or five hundred people and studies every detail of their life and culture: in which he comes to know every member of the community personally' (1913, 7). Torday and Hilton-Simpson had hardly done this.

Their longest stays had been amongst the Sungu section of the Tetela in the area of Mokunji and the related Olemba, Vungi, Okale and Lohinde Jofu in the *domain privé*; and in two Kuba areas – those at Misumba, the centre of the Ngongo, and at the Bushoong capital of Nsheng – with further information gathered from the Ngeende on a short trip from Misumba and notes made around Lusambo on the Isambo, a people only distantly related to the Kuba. In total they spent approximately four months each among the various Tetela and Kuba groups with the longest single stop, one of about ten weeks, at Nsheng. By contrast the account of peoples such as the Songye were made on only the briefest of acquaintance, apparently as short as a few days, and the report of the Topoke (Torday 1911e; Torday and Joyce 1922) resulted from discussions with a soldier from the area which being well to the north they had no opportunity to visit for themselves. Among the other groups surveyed in this more perfunctory way were the Boma, Nkutshu, Ohindu, Akela, Songo Meno, Mbuun, Pende, Lele, Wongo and Chokwe.

The skeletal nature of the resulting ethnography, of course, does not mean that the ethnographic collections formed were not in some cases impressive – the range of figures and masks collected from the Songye of Batempa is the obvious example. 'The local Basonge chief [presumably a chief of the Tempa section of the Songye], having heard of our presence and of our desire to purchase articles of native manufacture, came in one morning bringing a large number of interesting objects for sale', Hilton-Simpson recalled (1911, 35). In other words, the collection was formed outside the context of fieldwork. Given such circumstances, it is not surprising that the associated documentation is of limited value when placed beside the quality of the supporting information on the Kuba collection, or even the collections made at Mokunji amongst the so-called southern Tetela, neighbours of Batempa's Songye.

Yet, even if the model of the expedition's work was still ethnographic survey rather than intensive anthropology, an adjunct of travel rather than longer-term residence, its emphasis was shifting significantly in the direction Rivers implied. Certainly the attitude to knowledge, to 'facts', engendered by the use of the questionnaire technique, to some extent remained. Indeed, for many of the peoples visited the information sent back was organised into predetermined categories as had been the practice in the Kwilu. Joyce had simply to annotate Torday's notes, add appropriate remarks derived from his library researches, and send the text off to the printer. For Torday, however, the trick in the field was to find the most authoritative font of local wisdom and tap into that source. The photograph of Torday in deep discussion with the Bilumbu – a photograph taken at Misumba among the Kuba-Ngongo – illustrates the process: it seems likely that the 'Bilumbu', in Torday's orthography, is the *bulaam*, a Kuba title applied to experts in narrative traditions, local chroniclers – 'official historians' in Torday's explanation (1925a, 86–8; see also Vansina 1978, 17). The trustworthiness of the information was still Torday's predominant concern – 'my notes are absolutely *true*; no leg-pulling was possible with me, I tell you that all information is exclusively derived from natives, and checked by other natives', Torday wrote of the results of his work among the Ngongo (15 April 1908). The authentic voice was the indigenous voice, unambiguous, yet as complete as possible in all its inflections.

Peoples of the Sankuru

Torday's first proper fieldwork of the expedition, undertaken in the early weeks of 1908, was amongst peoples he came to designate as the southern Tetela. The problem posed by the Tetela was rather similar to that of the Mbala who had provided Torday with his introduction to field ethnography, namely, who are the Tetela? The peoples he called by that name include groups with considerable differences in cultural practice; they occupy quite different terrain, Mokunji in the south being in open cultivated land, by contrast with the Equatorial Forests which are home

Wood figure. Songye. 1908.6–22.164. H. 56 cm. (Collected at Batempa.)

Wood figure with teeth inset into the face, a horn containing medicines, together with feathers set in the head and woven raffia covering the lower body. Songye. 1908.6–22.159. H. 45 cm. (Collected at Okitulonga, on the Sankuru.)

to the northern Tetela; and there even seemed to be clearly identifiable physical distinctions between northern and southern groups in terms of skin colour and stature (Torday 1921, 372).

The term 'Tetela' itself has a confused etymology. The Sungu claimed it was a term given to them by the Arabs whose incursions into this part of Central Africa were brought to a halt by the battles between Arab and Congo State forces fought out in this very region with the active participation of Tetela auxiliaries on both sides. Torday later revised this assertion of the origin of the term suggesting the Arabs themselves had learnt it from the Malela (1921, 372), the most Arabised of the Tetela sub-groups; it was therefore an older appellation. He preferred the explanation given to him by the Olemba sub-group who linked it with the name of a deity

Wood mask (*moadi*) with red and white surface and the remains of a crest of feathers across the top. Tetela-Sungu, and in a style diverging from that illustrated in col. pl. I. 1908.6–22.132. H. 42 cm. (Collected at Kasongo.)

and offered as a translation either 'he who laughs not' or 'he at whom one may not laugh'. There were even supposed Tetela groups who eschewed the term Tetela altogether – like the Sungu on whom, ironically, Torday readily admitted he relied for the bulk of his information on Tetela culture. However, although elsewhere Torday rejected the name given to a people by foreigners in favour of the name they use of themselves in this case he retained it. Others have followed his example preferring to include the Sungu as part of the Tetela rather than as a separable ethnic group, which, on Torday's own evidence, was arguably the position in 1908.

For the sake of description Torday adopted the same procedure as he had amongst the Mbala in talking of separate but related northern and southern populations (Torday 1910a and b, 1921; Torday and Joyce 1922 and the typescript of 1910 from which it derives; and Hilton-Simpson 1911). As with so many similar situations where an available ethnographic description and administrative convenience combine to substantiate a particular version of ethnicity, the Sungu may now present themselves as unalterably Tetela. In the first accounts, however, they were represented as the most removed in culture and geography from the Tetela heartlands in the forests to the north. And what is true of ethnographic description in general is also true of art history – that the received wisdom on the Tetela may be derived from the least, not the most typical, source.

Take, for example, the mask collected by Torday which is often pointed to as characteristically Tetela (col. pl. 1) – as such it was published by Fagg (1965, 106), an evocation of the view that art styles are as definitive an index of ethnic identity as any other cultural feature; and the same opinion is implied by Felix who includes the mask as one of several Tetela types (1987, 175:4). Both authors certainly acknowledge the Tetela-Sungu source of the piece as part of the provenance. The mask is one of two that Torday collected in a closely similar, if not entirely identical, style. It was thought so impressive that it was immediately placed on exhibition when received in the British Museum, thus escaping the usual registration procedures. The authority for treating it as Sungu, however, is unassailable – it comes ultimately from Torday and Joyce who included it as such in their ethnographic account (1922, 77). The second mask, however, was collected at Batempa among the Songye and has been published as such (1922, 29) – though Felix has been misled into attributing it too to the Tetela (1987, 175:8). This strongly suggests that the associations of Sungu art – even though it is represented as prototypically Tetela – are to be sought among the peoples of the upper Sankuru, not among the Tetela to the north. Indeed, the northern Tetela do not seem to have masking traditions at all.

This conclusion helps explain another puzzle. Writing in 1910 Torday explained: 'No anthropomorphic fetishes are found among the Batetela, and all so-called fetishes seen in Museums are merely fancy carvings; true fetishes are procured from the official magicians, and the owners cannot be induced to part with them at any price' (1910a, 31). Even so, Torday did collect three 'Tetela' figures, all with bundles of 'fetish' attached to them and considerable evidence of extensive local use – these are not mere exercises in the skills of the carver induced by the purchasing power of acquisitive outsiders. Stylistically, they belong with the Songye, and two were acquired at Kasongo, the nearest Sungu settlement to the Songye at Tempa on the Sankuru. Again a statement applicable to the Tetela in general does not hold for the Sungu. Using Torday's own evidence, the case for considering the Sungu as a separate people from other Tetela groups, rather then describing Tetela culture through the lens of Sungu ethnography, is strong. Why, then, did Torday, and for that matter his *alter ego* Joyce, resist it?

It is an indication of how their interests were developing that they should select as a frame of description a perceived historical situation in preference to contemporary realities. Their thesis was that the Sungu had spear-headed a migration of related peoples from the north. They alone had moved completely out of the forests. Here they had been transformed, both through the need to adapt to a changed environment and through their increasing contacts with other savannah dwellers, Arabs and Portuguese. The northern Tetela retained the greatest range of original cultural fea-

Wood female figure with copper inlaid over the eyes, nose and forehead. From the settlement of Lusambo, and identified by Torday as Kuba (i.e. the Kuba-related Isambo). However, the influence of carving styles associated with the western Songye, some of whom also lived in the region of Lusambo, is also evident. 1908.Ty157. H. 22 cm.

tures; they alone remained rooted in the environmental circumstances in which their society had been forged. Thus, where the northern Tetela retained the use of raffia clothing and skins, the Sungu now wore the cotton trade cloth brought from the far side of Lake Tanganyika; the rectangular huts of the forests were replaced in the south by large circular structures, except where European architectural forms were beginning to be copied; social organisation was broadly similar, but there were considerable differences in attitudes to morality, in the treatment of miscreants and of slaves, in laws of inheritance, marriage and the treatment of the dead; and differing agricultural practice also produced variations in diet.

The concern in the earlier papers on the ethnography of the Kwilu had been with the sequence in which various groups had arrived in their present locations, and whence they had come. The perspective had been a regional one. However, by including the Sungu with the northern Tetela, and insisting on their relatedness despite the contradictory ethnography, a different emphasis emerged. It seemed possible to track the trajectory of a particular historical migration through space. Haddon, in commenting on Torday's first presentation of the results of the expedition, had remarked that 'the whole problem of the effect of environment on man has never yet been thoroughly studied, and it is one to which travellers should pay more attention in the future' (1910, 55). The Tetela seemed to allow an examination of the process in microcosm with elements of their changing culture spread out like the trail left by a plane.

The crucial moment was the leaving of the forest for the life of the savannah; it was like emerging from the clouds. One detail seemed to illustrate graphically some of the implications – the old problem that the word 'Tetela' was not known to the Sungu as a term for 'god'. In fact, it had been replaced by the word Winya, also meaning 'sun'. Once gripped by the idea of this ancient migration, the conclusion (provided by Joyce) was clear: 'when the Sungu emerged from the ancestral forest, the original home of the Batetela, into the plains full of beneficent sunlight, a confusion arose in their minds between the supreme god and the luminary which was to play a much more important part in their lives than before' (1921, 376). Convenient and simplistic as such an explanation is, the shift of emphasis towards the mechanisms of historical experience is significant.

Kot aPe and the Kuba

Torday's first impressions of the Kuba were similarly from the detached fringes of their society. The Isambo, whom he visited in the area of Lusambo, had migrated to the south-east of the Kuba many generations previously (during the mid-seventeenth century in Torday's estimate). They no longer recognised the suzerainty of the Kuba king (the *nyim*), one of the crucial tests of incorporation into the kingdom. Indeed, although Torday rejected use of the term Kuba as of foreign origin, in reality there was no local term by which to comprise all the various sub-groups of the Kuba kingdom. They were 'the people of the king' (Vansina 1978, 4). The word 'Bushongo', Torday's preferred term for the Kuba state as a whole, is the name of the core group only, the Bushoong, in whom kingship is invested and in whose territory the capital lies. 'Bambala', the name he adopted for the central Kuba, is an alternative to Bushoong.

However, when it came to thinking of a title for the book Torday and Joyce were to write on the Kuba, Torday himself already had another title in mind – he wished to call it 'The Kingdom of Shamba the Great', a reference to Shyaam aMbul aNgoong, the founder of the ruling Bushoong dynasty, 'King Alfred and Harun Al Rashid and Charlemagne all in one person' (1925a, 142). Torday found the *bulaam* of the Ngongo sub-group engaging, and was excited by the quality of both the information he recorded and the collection he formed; but he was quite simply enchanted by Shyaam's descendant, the Bushoong and thus the Kuba ruler, Kot aPe (or Kwete Peshanga Kena, as Torday rendered his full name). Torday promised the king that he would include some form of dedication to the royal dynasty in his writings on Kuba art and society – and, although his suggested title did not survive Joyce's editorial contribution to the ethnographic monograph they finally wrote (Torday and Joyce 1911), he did in due course inscribe his own autobiographical account of the Kasai expedition with an acknowlegement 'To the memory of Kwete' (1925a).

Nowadays it is not uncommon for anthropologists to express their indebtedness to their main contacts in whichever community they have worked. Indeed, there are some relationships engendered in the course of fieldwork that have come to be justly celebrated in the literature: that between Marcel Griaule and his Dogon collaborator, Ogotemmêli, in 1947 is probably the best known in an African context (Griaule 1948; Clifford 1983). Torday's friendship several decades earlier with Kot aPe is of similar

Kot aPe and his court as photographed in Nsheng.

Kuba-Ngongo chief in 'dance costume'.

importance. He was among the first ethnographers to make such a public declaration of gratitude to his native contacts.

Torday got off to a good start: he arrived with an unusual gift for the Nyim, sufficient to ensure his own standing as an exceptional visitor. This was a live crested eagle which he had purchased from an agent of the Kasai Company, with a wing spread of almost two metres (1925a, 131). Eagle plumes, as Torday had learnt from his Ngongo informants, are reserved to certain title holders including the king. His present attracted many admirers, and many courtiers sought the honour of providing it with food. Thus began a rather awkward series of presentations in which the Nyim sought to give Torday, among other gifts, items for his growing ethnographic collection; they were all significant objects which Torday had otherwise expressed a willingness to purchase. At the same time he was acquiring material from other Kuba at high cost, as he had also done among the outlying Kuba peoples he had visited: 'I am working strenuously on my bankruptcy', he had written from Misumba (6 March 1908) on the prices he was obliged to pay for a large Ngongo collection; 'I am now left absolutely destitute', he confided on leaving the Bushoong (4 January 1909). The embarrassment caused by the king's gesture was interpreted by Torday as evidence of his essential kindliness and humanity. The Nyim asked Torday for trifling items like boxes of matches in order, he later admitted, to give the impression that the process was two-way.

In letters Torday described Kot aPe in the same terms as he had Hilton-Simpson – he too was 'a brick' (1 October 1908), 'more of a gentleman in one toe than the whole American mission' (a reference to American Presbyterian missionaries, 22 October 1908). In print Torday reported that the king was 'a most intelligent native gentleman' (1910a, 39) and 'the perfect gentleman' (1925a, 115). He was dignified and benign, he 'erred on the side of clemency' (113). Yet the very kindliness which attracted Torday can be interpreted differently. History, not least Kuba oral tradition, records the fact that it was Kot aPe who led the revolt of 1904 in which the Kuba sought to oppose further incursions into their country by the State authorities. The event took place not long after the new king's succession (which was in 1902). In Torday's account, the king is portrayed as having been a most reluctant insurrectionist, forced into it against his own judgement in deference to the wishes of his people. Thus when, in 1908, an American missionary, Morrison, informed Count de Grunne, the officer in charge of the area, that another uprising was being planned, Torday from his vantage point at the capital itself hotly denied it. 'J'y suis, j'y reste', he replied. He saw in the event an attempt to depose the king and replace him with an alternative candidate.

In that he might well have been right; but whether the rumour emanated from the American mission alone or, quite possibly, was passed on from a source within the Kuba court itself is not discussed by Torday. He himself remained loyal to a particularly rosy view of Kuba society and the inviolability of the king's position, and he guessed that the missionaries were looking to find a more amenable channel through which to introduce the Christian message – that they, in effect, were perpetrating the calumny. But whatever the truth of these incidents, what is clear is that, divine king or not, Kot aPe was a central player in the politics of the court, not above them. Kot aPe's political opponents may equally have interpreted the subtlety and humanity attributed by Torday to the king as indecision.

In the course of research in the 1950s Jan Vansina was still able to reconstruct something of the extent to which Torday was influenced by the interests of the varying parties at court (Vansina 1978, 79). Certainly Torday and Hilton-Simpson cannot have escaped becoming embroiled in the intricacies of the Kuba political system. Unlike Griaule, who reported specifically on his conversations with Ogotemmêli, Torday in fact built up a picture of Kuba culture from extensive discussions with a wide range of courtiers and members of the royal household. He may not have had the length of residence Rivers later recommended as necessary for intensive field research, and he may have chosen to live in the capital town of the kingdom rather than a smaller-scale community, but Torday did 'get to know personally' the more restricted society of the court; and, although his account is to a degree king-centred, he was very aware of the tensions in Kuba political life.

Vansina also remarks (1978, 229) that Torday does not mention the fact that Kot aPe's heir apparent, who eventually succeeded to the throne in 1916 as Mbop aMbweeky, had already been designated by 1908. Yet whilst it is not extensively discussed in his more ethnographical writing,

Torday certainly made clear in his popular account that he not only knew of the heir apparent's presence at court (he talks of the title of heir apparent under the name 'Buimbi') but even identified him as one of the leaders of the very faction in Kuba society seeking most vigorously to resist foreign incursions, contrary to the inclinations of the king (1925a, 116–17). Indeed, in order not to restrict his contacts with the king and his immediate entourage Torday was also engaged in a series of more secretive gift exchanges with the king's political opponents. It is perhaps the greatest indication of Torday's diplomatic skills that he managed not only to bridge the gap between the king and contrary elements within the court but also to be himself exempted from the normal hostility inspired by foreigners. Indeed, in the relatively short time he was at Nsheng, he was sufficiently trusted to be admitted to court title without apparently its being a matter of controversy. His title was 'Migenja', a version of an alternative name for the capital.

It was from the heir apparent that Torday acquired an important backrest carved with a ram's head, the ram being an image restricted to royalty. This was given under instruction of the king. Of all the objects collected by Torday, however, it is the king figures which are best known. The story of their acquisition throws into greater relief the extent of Torday's awareness of the complexities of the Kuba court. Field collecting, when it is done properly as part of field research, is often instructive. Seeking to acquire something, after all, obliges someone to own it; but establishing exactly who is rarely simple. Groups as extensive as a clan, or larger, may have some form of interest in the object. Determining ownership can be a somewhat artificial act; establishing adequate recompense is thus in itself a form of ethnographic research.

From the start Torday made it plain that in addition to seeking to record Kuba history and culture in order to place it amongst the annals of important civilisations (where he was already convinced it belonged) he was also collecting objects to ensure their preservation. The report of Torday's explanation to the king is given by Hilton-Simpson: '"Often," said Torday, "you give away some keepsake to a white man, but what becomes of it? It is lost, or in years to come no one will know what it is or whence it came. Everything that you or your people will sell to me will go to the big house I have mentioned, and there remain for all time as evidence of the skill and greatness of your race." Thus he explained to the chief the uses of the British Museum' (1911, 193–4).

We are told, and there is every reason to accept it, that Kot aPe took to this project with enthusiasm. Certainly he gave Torday a number of important objects. A carved ivory tusk associated with Shyaam is in this category, as is one of the king figures he acquired, which putting together

Wood backrest surmounted by a carved ram's head. Kuba-Bushoong. 1909.5–13.9. H. 36 cm. (Collected at Nsheng.)

Wood figure (*ndop*) commemorating MishaaPelyeeng aNce as indicated by the drum associated with his reign carved on the plinth. Kuba-Bushoong. 1909.5–13.2. H. 55.5 cm. (Collected at Nsheng.)

information from letters and published sources (principally Joyce 1925) we know to have been that commemorating Kot aMbul given to Torday by Kot aPe as a present the day before he and Hilton-Simpson finally left Nsheng. The figure passed from Torday either directly or indirectly into the hands of a territorial administrator, Blondeau, to the Musée Royal de l'Afrique Centrale at Tervuren in Belgium, and thence back to the Musées Nationaux du Zaire in Kinshasa (Cornet 1982, 105).

There are considerable discrepancies between the various accounts of how many such king figures Torday saw, which they were, and even how many he collected (see Mack forthcoming). Three figures acquired by Torday are now in the British Museum, those associated with Shyaam aMbul aNgoong, MishaaPelyeeng aNce and Mbop Pelyeeng aNce. Despite what has sometimes been said, we now know that all three were acquired by purchase and the figure of Kot aMbul was unique in being a gift. This required great personal expense for they were obtained through the Kuba court. We have no confirmation that the king himself accepted any personal recompense. Certainly Torday tried to have a replica made of the figure of Shyaam to be sent to the king as his own way of acknowledging the significance of the figure to the royal dynasty, though whether this ever happened is not recorded.

The Kuba collection

The king figures (*ndop*) commemorate particular rulers: they are 'spirit doubles', encapsulating the principles of kingship as devolved upon a particular ruler. Rubbing them with oil preserves the spirit of royalty at the heart of the kingdom when the king is physically absent from his capital; sleeping with them incubates an incoming ruler into the spiritual aspects of his new role (Vansina 1972; Maesen 1967, 36). Even though Torday saw at most only five examples, a small enough conspectus from which to judge, he considered all the king figures to be portraits done from life and thus datable to the reign of the king represented. That would make the figure of Shyaam (*cover*) of seventeenth-century origin and thus amongst the oldest complete examples of African wood sculpture. This is what he understood from his Kuba informants, and, as always, he was disposed to accept the authority of what looked like an authentic indigenous view.

There are, however, clear stylistic grounds for doubting that in this instance his trust was justified; and in any case the sense in which they 'represent' individual rulers is a highly specialised one. What associates the figures to particular kings is not the figure itself, but the presence of a small emblem carved on the integral plinth at the base of the sculpture, each one different and identified with the reign of an individual ruler. The figure of Shyaam is still of considerable antiquity in an African context; but it is likely to have been carved at approximately the same time as the other two in the British Museum, and, according to one probable line of reasoning (Rosenwald 1974), all to be the work of the same carver. They would seem to date to the second half of the eighteenth century, though in which decade remains undecided (Vansina 1978, 213–15).

Kot aPe with four Songye charms he had in his possession at Nsheng.

Opposite Wood figure (*ndop*) commemorating Mbop Pelyeeng aNce. He was renowned as an accomplished iron-worker as indicated by the (now broken) representation of an anvil, or better, an anvil stand, at the front of the sculpture. Kuba-Bushoong. 1909.5–13.1. H. 55 cm. (Collected at Nsheng; the third king figure collected for the British Museum is reproduced on p. 16 and on the cover.)

The idea of the king figures as a kind of spiritual repository and their historicity clearly take the *ndop* beyond the domain of individual ownership; they were to an extent common property. They were also in a different category from, for instance, the royal charms (figures in the Songye style acquired by Kot aPe himself) upon which the king's magical powers in part rested. Torday was allowed to photograph the royal charms, but he did not seek to collect them. Whereas the king figures were sculpture associated with powerful people, an adjunct to kingly power but not a direct source of it, the charms were powerful objects in themselves, infused with magical properties. The removal of the royal charms might have been conceived as diminishing royal authority.

This is not to say that acquiring the king figures did not involve a level of intervention in the Kuba political process, but it was of a different order from what might have been implied in acquiring the royal charms. Indeed, it was the king himself who suggested the appropriate strategy for acquiring the king figures, which Torday's letters indicate he had not been at all sure he would be allowed to do. The king further pointed out that his political opponents would be more enthusiastic about Torday acquiring the figures if it was thought that he, the king, opposed the idea. Torday's off-hand comment on the procedure – 'there never was such lavish bribery, so much coaxing, such abject flattery' (1925a, 150) – does not alter the fact that Torday, alone of those who collected king figures in the opening years of the century, took some account of problems of communal ownership in recompensing a large number of courtiers, though not all knew what was happening. If he had been disposed to see the Kuba court as a cosy club, these machinations made him aware of underlying tensions.

The rest of the substantial collection formed amongst the Bushoong was similarly acquired with due attention to local protocol. Even in his dealings with the less elevated members of Kuba society Torday refrained from using

his influence with the court to his own advantage. 'We paid good prices;' Torday recalled, 'when our offer did not come up to the seller's expectation he knew that he could carry his goods away without fear that we might use our influence with the great men of the country to put pressure on him to part with them against his wishes' (1925a, 193). Hilton-Simpson was less certain that Torday had not gone too far in his wish to be fair; a letter to Joyce on the subject gave him an opportunity to display his liking for the exclamation mark: 'Of course some of the things are treasured heirlooms etc and have to be paid for "through the nose" after much bargaining, the prices being enormous, but the everyday sorts of things are very dear too. The most expensive articles are those given us for nothing! The exchange of presents to cement friendship invariably leaves the Bakuba with the best of the deal!' (16 November 1908).

Nowadays fieldworkers are often advised against acquiring examples of local arts at an excessive price as this will only encourage unrealisable expectations on the part of those amongst whom they are working. In Torday's time, however, what Europeans valued in the products of the Congo State were natural substances, ivory and rubber, not artefacts. Ironically the only object on which he was obliged to pay duty by the Congo authorities was the ivory tusk given to him by Kot aPe. As Hilton-Simpson's remark on the expensive 'gift' illustrates, collecting and field-work were thoroughly intertwined – both progressed in tandem to the extent that confidence and trust were engendered. Even so, Torday was rare, indeed, in spending the rapidly diminishing resources of the expedition on objects whilst knowingly allowing the Kuba consistently to get the better of the transactions.

In its totality the Kuba collection formed in 1908 provides a useful contrast with the earliest collections Torday had made firstly in the Lake Mweru area and especially in his subsequent work in the Kwilu. There the emphasis was on a view of authenticity which stressed the magical properties of the physical compound *kisi* above the various magical devices to which it was applied: this could be readily justified on anthropological grounds. Now, however, authenticity had been confidently recast as an aspect of antiquity. The oldest object, like the oldest authoritative inform-ant, provided the most faithful representation of the state of a culture. Torday would not have understood the current interest of the very British Museum Department which houses his collection in documenting such phenomena as the recycling by craftsmen in developing countries of European waste products like tin cans, motor parts or tyres.

One of the objects which Torday most valued was a fragment of an old drum which he described as '*a marvel*' (28 November 1908), and which Hilton-Simpson said was 'the finest carving yet collected' (24 November 1908), despite the fact that by then two king figures had already been acquired. The drum, only half of it still intact but its surface covered with the intricate network of carved pattern which is characteristic of Kuba art, is said to date from the reign of MboMboosh, Shyaam's successor but one. If true, it would be of seventeenth-century origin. By contrast, Torday collected very few masks amongst the Bushoong. His reason was that he

Fragment of an old drum. Kuba-Bushoong. 1909.5–13.265. H. 99 cm. (Collected at Nsheng.)

Mwaash aMbooy masker
photographed among the Kuba-
Bushoong. The mask is one of several
types collected by Torday.

considered masking a recent innovation amongst the central Kuba, and
of Kete origin. He did not, therefore, consider masks an appropriate representation of Bushoong culture. Only four examples of masks were collected
to give a type series. Authenticity was defined in terms of historical value
– but then for Torday and Joyce anthropology had emerged as historical
science.

The ideal of personal involvement

Torday confided that he felt the research he had conducted amongst the
Kuba was the best he had done – 'you will think me a conceited ass,' he
wrote to Joyce, 'but I am very proud of the result of my researches here'
(4 December 1908). On leaving Nsheng he went on to tell Joyce: 'There
is no man alive who knows as much about the Bakuba as we do; so at
least says the chief; for "I have told you all I know and spoken to you

as no Bushongo ever spoke to a white man; the old have told you more than they would tell even to me; you are in all the secrets of our people"' (17 December 1908).

These comments mark a recognition of the shift which had taken place in Torday's experience of ethnography. The enthusiasm for data collection was still there. But the controls on objectivity represented by the questionnaire, the camera and the phonograph no longer seemed sufficient in themselves; they were props to be wheeled into place when circumstances, whether language difficulties or shortage of time, prevented other forms of relationship from developing. Knowledge, 'facts', could not be advanced as objective merely because they were impersonal, acquired in a rigid and controlled way. Indeed, in Torday's work among the Kuba the various artificial aids to objectivity had been overtaken by a style and quality of relationship which was at once personalised and intimate. The care and diplomacy with which Torday felt he had conducted all his dealings with the Kuba signalled these changes. Fieldwork implies the creation of relationships and responsibilities; and the most profound insight, it now seemed, was to be derived from the closest relationships. The questionnaire had its limitations – it was not a rule book; it could not tell you how to create trust.

It is also revealing that in none of the various accounts of his work amongst the Kuba did Torday revert to the methods of the adventure-story writer. The wiles of bushcraft had come to seem somehow inappropriate; after all, they were to an extent the 'tricks' of the trade, and as such inconsistent with the esteem in which Torday had come to regard the Kuba. If at times he appears to us conspiratorial, he none the less presents his conspiracies as aspects of his engagement with Kuba society and its complex polity; there is little sense that he set out to hoodwink naïve hosts. This was, however, a refinement of style and approach Torday reserved to the Kuba. 'Bushcraft' returned when Torday left the Kasai to undertake a crossing of the terrain lying to the west, the unexplored, 'hostile' territory between the Loange River and the Kasai occupied by the Wongo, the Lele and some groups of the Chokwe.

To an extent, both Torday and Hilton-Simpson independently assure us (Torday 1910a, 50; Hilton-Simpson 1911, 320–3), they were able to survive the traversing of this difficult country precisely because Torday came to be regarded as a great trickster. He had earlier written asking Joyce to procure for him from Hamley's store a number of clockwork elephants which marched along with trunks waving when they were wound up. By displaying these with considerable theatricality Torday was quickly credited with exceptional powers. At least, he pointed out, like this they were able to travel without resort to firearms. Yet from the point of view of ethnography it can hardly be said to be an immense advantage to bear a reputation for extraordinary feats of magic. Torday acknowledged that this was not the most successful part of his whole expedition. In difficult circumstances he had done what he could: he had managed to form the first ethnographic collections from the area; he had sketched in an outline of the cultures of the region; but, in the end, he was to characterise

A Wongo chief with a whistle hung from his neck.

Torday demonstrating his clockwork elephant.

the exploration of the area immediately to the west of the Kasai as essentially of geographical rather than anthropological importance (1910a, 52). Torday may have recognised the positive advantage of direct intimate experience of a culture, the technique which came to characterise British and American ethnography, but he still saw its possibilities as a matter of local circumstance.

It can be argued that the Kuba were important to Torday, and the work he undertook amongst them important in the development of African studies and ethnographic writing generally, because the emphasis of their culture closely matched that of his research. The Kuba were temperamentally historians. Like many centralised states, theirs was a society obsessively interested in precedent; Torday, in the wake of the vagaries of evolutionary paradigms was similarly interested to document actual pre-existing conditions. More than that, what he learnt from the Kuba did not look like mere folklore. They could recount king lists (as recorded in Torday and Joyce 1910, 17–19), locate events in time by reference to the kings in whose reign they occurred – they even talked of a solar eclipse and a passage of Halley's comet, thus providing a means of linking Kuba chronology to historical time. Oral history was for Torday real history – history like the European historian might investigate. Memory was documentary.

Torday was always disposed to treat the evidence relayed to him by the senior spokesmen of any society as a literal representation of fact. This had even been so in his earlier period in the Kwilu. In discussing the king of the Yaka, for instance, Torday reports an oral account of a ruler who hauled himself up from a sitting position by stabbing knives into the backs of slaves (1913a, 144). This is not taken as a statement about wealth and the status of slaves but as an actual event, and Torday as a result calculated for us how many slaves would die by such means in a single day and, given the local price of slaves, what such a practice would cost over a year.

If perhaps no one would now be disposed to doubt Torday's acceptance of oral tradition as an authentic document, it would still be with considerable reservation. Oral tradition was in one sense often wrong. It has since become clear, for instance, that the Kuba king lists recorded by Torday are significantly flawed. What Torday was recording was not history as experienced but history as interpreted and reinterpreted. He failed to recognise this. Yet no more was Freud analysing dreams as they were dreamed by patients; he too was giving credence to what was remembered of the experience of dreams. Torday may not have had the intellectual sophistication to argue with his contemporary that what is perceived to be real is real. Oral tradition is an authentic document in an ethnographic rather than a strictly historical sense; nevertheless, treating the Kuba account of their past as reality already represented a considerable advance over an older tradition of treating native accounts of myth and history as illusion.

On completing his study of the Kuba-Ngongo Torday wrote to tell Joyce:

> There are many things those who may come after me may find but they will find all I wrote is strictly correct. Not a word of all written to this day has been obtained otherwise as from the native himself and all has been controlled with other members of the tribe; and I may say: I swear to have told the truth, all the truth, and nothing but truth (17 December 1908).

The aim was not to be the ventriloquist but the ventriloquist's dummy.* Among the Kuba Torday had discovered a voice that was dignified, regal, but above all one that seemed to be historically informed.

*Subsequent to writing this I have realised that I am echoing a phrase of a colleague who has made similar points in relation to the enterprise of art history in Africa (Picton 1986).

5 *Objects and ideas*

During the opening decades of the century the Ethnography Galleries of the British Museum were not perhaps the magnet for avant-garde artists that the Trocadero was in Paris – but then, art in Britain had not the same vigorous and developing avant-garde. Jacob Epstein was a rare exception. Having lived for three years in Paris, he moved to London in 1905. By 1912 he was conversant with the size and quality of the Museum's collections from Polynesia and Africa (Bassani and McLeod n.d., 26). Yet as an artist Epstein still looked to associate himself as much with what was happening in Paris as with his British contemporaries – at least until Wyndham Lewis helped to found the Vorticist movement in Britain shortly before the outbreak of the First World War. Interestingly, in the artistic community in Britain it was principally sculptors, Epstein and later Henry Moore, who were the leading enthusiasts of non-Western art, whilst in France it was mainly painters.

Of the Paris-based artists André Derain was one of the few to be aware of the riches of the British Museum. He visited London on several occasions in the opening decade of the century and is known to have spent time looking at African material in Bloomsbury. He wrote to the France-based artist Maurice de Vlaminck in 1906 during his second trip across the Channel: 'I am moved by my trips to London, to the Musée National [the British Museum] as well as the Musée nègre [the Ethnography Galleries]. This [African] art is wonderful, full of expression . . . these are forms created in the open, in bright light, and they are meant to be seen in bright light' (1955, 197). It followed that the interplay of light and form was a consideration in their creation. The illumination of the darkness in this sense, however, was essentially a discovery made in continental Europe. In Britain the new insights to which Torday contributed had less to do with the inspiration and example of African art as with the subtleties and expressions of African culture generally. This implied a different kind of interest in objects; but it also involved an interest in objects of different kinds from those which fired the artistic imagination in France.

Roger Fry is often cited as one of the first British writers about art to take an interest in its 'primitive' manifestations. In practice what he had to say is contained in only five pages, the text of a talk given at the Athenaeum after he had seen African sculpture displayed in a small exhibition at the Chelsea Book Club. However, the opening sentences of the volume in which his discussion of 'primitive' art occurs arguably give a

Raffia textile with cut-pile embroidery. The colours are red, black and yellow. This example is from the Shoowa, a northern sub-group of the Kuba living just to the south of the Kasai River. Torday did not visit the heartlands of the Shoowa and may have collected this and other examples along the River itself. Kuba-Shoowa. 1979.Af1.2675. w. 56 cm.

better impression than does his short essay, 'Negro Sculpture', of how informed opinion in Britain was coming to regard African art:

> When we look at ancient works of art we habitually treat them not merely as objects of aesthetic enjoyment but also as successive deposits of the human imagination. It is indeed this view of works of art as crystallised history that accounts for much of the interest in ancient art by those who have but little aesthetic feeling (1920, 1).

Kuba art was of importance firstly because it was demonstrably old, and also because for those museum visitors without the well-honed perception of the artistic élite it was accessible. Its emphasis on decoration and its apparent tendency in figurative sculpture towards more directly represen-tational imagery were undemanding. It seemed that it could be accom-modated within existing European taste and expectation. Richly patterned raffia-pile cloth similar to that still produced by the Kuba had been collected from the mouth of the Congo River as early as the sixteenth century. It had been appreciated as an African example of 'velours', velvet. Techni-cally, however, it is actually different. The exploration of pattern, highlighted by the adroit use of contrasting colours, suggested an innova-tive and experimental artistic practice in contrast to the repetitive imagery expected of cultures seen as weighed down by conservative tradition.

Kuba king figures, because of their representational qualities, were dis-cussed by Torday and Joyce (and displayed in the Ethnography Galleries) as portraiture. Great pains were taken to point out the distinctions between the hands of artists who, if the figures had been 'portraits' done from life, must have carved the three figures in the British Museum in quite different reigns. Unfortunately, this too is highly debatable. None the less, its representational idiom was challenging. African art had been held to be incapable of such developments. In the absence of other evidence abstrac-tion or more interpretative rendering of human subjects often appeared to popular sensibilities as the resort of the artistically unaccomplished. Kuba art, especially if the sculpture had, as was thought, been produced to a consistent level over many generations, implied a practised mastery of materials and an exceptional culture.

Kuba art, in fact, looked unAfrican; it dealt in the exploration of geo-metric pattern and in rounded figurative sculpture. Yet it came from one of the continent's remotest corners. The corollary was the odd fact that the art conventionally thought of as prototypically African often came from areas exposed to substantially greater external influence than the Kasai. Exploring the implications of this irony was one of the tasks to which Torday turned his attention in the last decades of his life.

When he returned to England in 1909, however, Torday did not foresee that his involvement with field anthropology might be at an end or that he might metamorphose from a talented fieldworker into an anthropo-logist. Unlike the brief period of uncertainty in 1907 – when he returned to London contemplating a career in colonial administration but was per-suaded back to Central Africa – he now definitely wanted to undertake a further expedition as soon as practicable. This time he hoped to revisit the south-east of the Belgian Congo where he had been in the first years of the century. Funding from a variety of sources was anticipated – perhaps through the British Museum or another British institution, perhaps from a Hungarian foundation, as Torday's achievements were beginning to receive some recognition in his country of origin. He was even willing to accept 'a helpful hand stretched across the ocean by a Yankee' (20 April 1909).

He received much encouragement. In 1910 the Emperor of Austria conferred upon him the Imperial gold medal for Science and Art; his address to the Royal Geographical Society on the work of the expedition was well received by a distinguished audience including Sir H.H. Johnston, Balfour and Haddon; and the Trustees of the British Museum formally thanked him for his efforts and presented him with a set of catalogues. Later, in 1912, they also purchased and gave him a cast of a Congo chief. Torday was elected to the Council of the Royal Anthropological Institute and served for many years. Despite these acts of recognition, however, the proposed expedition never took place. Indeed, he was, it seems, never to visit Africa again.

Towards the end of his life he was to become deeply embroiled in a study of documentary sources on African history and ethnography for which his field experience and his prodigious linguistic talents ideally fitted him, and which resulted in the publication just before his death of the substantial volume entitled *Descriptive Sociology: African Races* (1930a). First, however, the results of the 1907–9 work had to be published. Though the ethnographic reports (principally those published as Torday and Joyce 1911 and 1922) are voluminous, they were already well advanced in draft form shortly after the turn of the new decade. Since the work had been undertaken under the auspices of the authorities in Brussels, and the mission had received official government recognition, the results were to be published in Belgium and in French. 'The Kingdom of Shamba the Great' came out less portentously as *Les Bushongo* within a year, and a typescript, which is substantially the English draft of that part of the 1922 publication which deals with the Tetela, Songye, Akela and the Topoke, was already prepared by December 1910. The speed with which two such large volumes had been got ready confirms the orderliness and completeness of the notes provided from the field by Torday. Indeed, the *Handbook* of the British Museum's ethnographic collections which was first published in 1910 drew heavily on Torday's work in its Central African section and included illustrations of objects which had only just been collected by Torday.

An early impression of the significance that the 1907–9 collection, and especially that part from the Kasai, was to have, can be gauged from Joyce's comments on an Ngongo cup collected by Torday and published before he and Hilton-Simpson returned from the field. Firstly the evidence of wear indicated 'that the cup is a genuine "antique" in the limited sense of antiquity which can be applied to objects from savage Africa' (1909, 2) – in other words, it crept into Fry's criterion of objects to interest the viewer

Wood cup. Said to be amongst the
most ancient objects still extant at
the time of its collection. Kuba-
Ngongo. 1908.Ty78. H. 12.5 cm.
(Collected at Misumba.)

without at the same time challenging his aesthetic preconceptions. Yet
it was a puzzle. 'On the whole the shape of the vessel distinctly suggests
European influence, just as the ornamented body suggests the art of Benin.
But it is impossible to find in this neighbourhood even the remotest traces
of direct European influence earlier than the comparatively recent date
of Wissmann's visit' (1909, 2).

From the vantage point of the Pitt-Rivers Museum, Oxford – also a bene-
ficiary of Torday's collecting – Henry Balfour, in reviewing Torday and
Joyce's volume *Les Bushongo*, reiterated the point, again taking off from
the baseline provided by the remarkable arts of Benin: 'If the punitive
expedition to Benin astonished the ethnological world by the revelation
of the marvellous *cire perdu* bronze-work and the ivory carving of that
Nigerian district, Mr. Torday's expedition to the Bushongo reveals a yet
more wonderful art-culture, the more to be admired since it is strictly indigenous and uninfluenced by contact with Europeans' (1912, 47). Torday
himself conceded that as far as the Bushoong are concerned, Shyaam is
reputed in tradition to have travelled widely beyond Kuba territory; but
he said nothing to dent the unanimity which was emerging – 'the most
un-African shapes are found amongst tribes related to the Bushongo [he
is referring to the Wongo and Lele], who have never been under the influence of the traveller king, and who are the most conservative and most
averse to strangers of all people I have ever met' (1911c, 46).

Wood enema with carved human head. Kuba-Bushoong 1909.5–13.112. L. 23 cm. (Collected at Nsheng.)

The implications of this view are large. Firstly, in advance of the diffusionist debates which were to rage in British anthropology after the First World War this was to set down an important marker. Torday and Joyce did cast a conjectural glance at the broader affinities of Kuba culture and came up with some highly speculative conclusions about the remoter origins of at least some elements in the complex that constitutes Kuba society. They noted similarities with the northern parts of the Equatorial Forest in isolated aspects of material culture – objects of divination and a throwing knife, then already extinct amongst the Kuba. They identified the ultimate homeland of the Kuba with a distant area in the region of Lake Chad. For the most part, however, they limited themselves in *Les Bushongo* and elsewhere to systematising Kuba chronicles as related to Torday.

This was a long way from anticipating the characteristic arguments of the emerging body of diffusionist literature. In the second and third decades of the century studies of the geographic distribution of everything from mummification to pearl fish-hooks were advanced as a means of tracing broad lines of human migration and the transmission of culture. The comparisons were often as uncritical as the evolutionist speculations which they were intended to replace. There was, as A.M. Hocart remarked (1954, 10), a 'cranky' element to all this. Grafton Elliot Smith, concerned to demonstrate the Egyptian origin of a megalithic culture complex, selected his evidence from all quarters of the globe. A monument found at the Mayan site of Copan seemed to portray on each of its four corners an Indian elephant complete with turbanned rider. To the converts to unicentric diffusion this was proof that Egyptian influence which had swept through India had even reached Central America (Elliot Smith 1924). Sceptics preferred to see in the monument a more likely subject, whether the representation of a tapir, a macaw, or even a tortoise.

For a review of Kuba art in broad diffusionist terms a modern commentary (Meurant 1986) gives a much better idea of the oddities of such a position than anything Torday wrote. Torday was never in favour of tracing distant sources for Kuba artistry, let alone the idea of the Egyptian grand tour, even in a more restricted form – the influence of Egypt on Bantu culture. Regarding the indigenous origins of ironworking in Africa, Torday wrote, 'no bronze implements have ever been found in Black Africa; had the Africans received iron from the Egyptians, bronze would have preceded this metal and all traces of it would not have disappeared' (1913d, 414). Beyond that he preferred to start from solid fact rather than speculation. F.W. Maitland had written 'by and by anthropology will have the choice between being history and being nothing' (1911, III, 259). His aim was to direct attention back to actual processes of development and the more verifiable events of the past – a goal partly realised in Rivers's *The History of Melanesian Society* (1914) but ultimately subverted in the diffusionist version of historical reconstruction.

Torday's main contribution to the question was his essay on 'The Influence of the Kingdom of Kongo on Central Africa' (1928a). One of his purposes was to try and explain 'the rise of a distinctive high civilisation [that of the Kuba] in the midst of peoples of much lower culture' (1928a, 159).

It is not by any means a theoretical tract but rather a search of the available historical and cultural sources to establish the merits of the Kuba tradition that Shyaam travelled extensively among peoples to the west of the Kasai. The historical kingdom of Kongo, documented in European sources going back to the late fifteenth century, provided a stimulating set of parallels both in terms of social and craft organisation, in titles and terminology, and in art and material culture. Torday concludes that there were significant levels of contact between the Kuba and the Kongo in the first part of the seventeenth century. He is careful, however, to leave the question as to how these contacts were achieved and what form they took for further work. He was prepared to regard the story of Shyaam himself journeying westwards as a metaphor rendered in Kuba idiom for contacts that may or may not have engaged the king personally. This was history in the sense Maitland had intended, a question of dates and chronologies, of events with the authority of written or oral testimony. There were question marks remaining: it was conjectural but it was not for all that 'conjectural history' in its Enlightenment sense, let alone its diffusionist form.

This – a number of years on from his first reflections with Joyce on the issue – was to water down the sense of the uniqueness of Kuba culture: the Kuba reflected the glories that were the old kingdom of Kongo. But it did not move to any greater assertion of European influence on Central African art. In fact, the arrival of European influence is portrayed as one of the factors contributing to the *decline* of the Kongo by comparison with the Kuba, protected by their relative isolation from extensive and corrupting external contacts.

The second point to emerge from the assertion of the entirely indigenous sources of Kuba art concerns the standing of African culture in European perceptions of what was still the 'Dark Continent'. The comparison constantly made with Benin is significant. There the arrival of the Portuguese had been seen as a highly significant moment in the development of its arts. Artistic excellence could be explained by exposure to European influence. Something similar occurred after the discovery of the immense walls and impressive architectural features at the site of Great Zimbabwe – for a long time that too was never attributed its true African origin.

In analysing Kuba art, however, Joyce had been able to detect 'no more than the merest shadow' of Portuguese influence. The image of so un-African an African society, patinated with approval in the writings of Torday, Joyce and others, was frankly unexpected. Its 'discovery' posed an awkward question. Perhaps the nearest equivalent in European thought is the imagined kingdom of Prester John. Yet that was a Christian African kingdom, a 'lost' culture once in touch with a world beyond Africa. There are echoes, perhaps, of a comparison of the kingdom of Shyaam and that of Prester John in some of Torday's discussion. He was initially inclined to make something of a Bushoong tale that cited a remote white ancestor. The point was taken up by Haddon: 'It is, to my mind, very suggestive that the most civilized, cultured, and artistic people in Central Africa should themselves own that hundreds of years ago there was a white ancestor somewhere behind them' (1910, 55). Torday himself was aware that some elements of Bushoong myth might also be suggestive: 'I am afraid', he wrote from the field, 'that people will say that the mythology of the Bakuba is a hash up of the Bible' (17 December 1908). But in the end Shyaam was not Prester John. Kuba art and culture might be exceptional, but it had to be faced: it was a purely African achievement.

To make the point the material as it was displayed in the Ethnographic

Wood stool, described in the Torday documentation as a royal throne. Kuba-Bushoong. 1909.5–13.3. H. 45 cm. (Collected at Nsheng.)

Galleries was somewhat different from expectation. The main method of exhibition in the British Museum as at the Pitt-Rivers and elsewhere had consistently been typological, serried ranks of objects arranged and classed by function, often on a continent-wide basis rather than as localised features. Arrows, combs, textiles, pottery – whether from the Congo Basin or not – all tended to get mixed in with equivalent objects from elsewhere in Africa. The Kuba material, however, was all displayed together. Large prints from Torday's field photographs were included, one of Kot aPe and his court, another of a Kuba elder, and a third of a courtier holding a king figure. The display invited attention to Kuba art as a handle on Kuba culture. In this instance at least the integrity of an artistic tradition was retained.

The view revealed by these display methods, as by Torday and Joyce's writings, also had political implications. Torday had as part of his official support both from the British Museum and the Congo State authorities been warned off too overt an interest in politics. He largely complied: indeed, for his part Hilton-Simpson went out of his way to remark that they had heard no tales of atrocities nor witnessed any in their travels (1911, ix). Torday, however, did write to Joyce to say that 'although, of course, no politics *can* enter into our book it seems to me that it ought to be pointed out that the Bushongo having been able to evolve a civilisation of their own, this true negro civilisation ought not to be destroyed even to make room for the European article; it ought to be rather developped [sic], eventually guided, but certainly encouraged' (4 December 1908). This may not have been an opinion to make headlines like those attending reports of atrocities, but it did represent an important shift in focus. Any tendency to justify colonial expansion or missionary effort with reference to a lingering belief in the tenets of social evolution could be challenged on the basis of the construction of Kuba culture. They were much more than romanticised noble savages. By their own efforts they had achieved 'civilisation'.

The theme was one to which Torday often returned in the decades to come. His autobiographical books are full of hints for the enlightened administrator in Africa. *Causeries Congolaises*, published in 1925, was specifically written to inspire in residents of the Belgian Congo a more appreciative attitude to Central African culture. And the point applied more generally throughout the continent. Torday concluded a public lecture in 1931 on 'The Things that Matter to the West African' with the reflection:

> Under the present impact with European influences Africa is pregnant
> with a new world and, if all goes well, will give birth to a new culture,
> truly African, but different from that of the past. It will borrow from
> Europe with discrimination that which is best and most appropriate to
> the African's natural environment and throw overboard many of the
> institutions he cherished in the past. If we want to collaborate in the
> shaping of the future we must, above all, study carefully and
> sympathetically his time-honoured customs, beliefs and institutions
> (1931b, 113).

A plea for paternalism rather than self-determination this may have been, but it derived from a strong belief in the independent potential and the self-sufficiency of traditional African culture. Not only did it not need European intervention to develop, European influence had often had the opposite effect; it had not been a consistent force for good. This, for Torday, was another of the lessons of Kuba art and history.

Some of the publications referred to here date from the decade of the 1920s. By then Torday's personal circumstances had changed substantially. Des-

A series of ceremonial knives and a fly whisk. Kuba-Bushoong. The largest (1909.5–13.192; L. 79.5 cm) was carried by the king only. (Collected at Nsheng.)

pite his earlier misgivings, Torday had finally married a British wife before the War and had a daughter. He was obliged to look for less adventurous, gainful employment. Thus in 1913 he accepted an invitation to examine and provide documentation for a Congo collection recently purchased by the University Museum, Philadelphia, to which Torday himself later provided material from his own private collection. The invitation must have pleased him – the bulk of the objects he was asked to investigate had been acquired, ill-documented, from Frobenius. He spent several months in

Philadelphia as curator and lecturer (Torday 1913b). On his return he set out on a new tack, that of a medical career. Having himself been gored by a rhinocerous, which left him in pain for much of the remainder of his life, he enrolled at the London Hospital as a student and passed the first stages of a degree course.

In 1914 Europe was launched into turmoil. Torday had a bad war. He was unwilling to return with his British family to Hungary, yet as a Hungarian citizen he was classed as an enemy alien. He was effectively interned in his house in London for the duration of the War, and with the restriction on his movements he was obliged to abandon his medical studies. The authorities of the British Museum made an attempt to get Torday out of the impasse by lending official support to an application for his naturalisation as a British citizen. From Joyce we learn that this failed 'due to a peculiar accident' (1932, 48). What the difficulty was is unclear. The British Museum Archives record details of an elaborate scheme devised by Sir Hercules Read (report to Trustees dated 4 November 1916) to send Torday to China. Sir Hercules had learnt of a large quantity of Chinese ceramics and bronzes uncovered in the course of railway construction. The leading collector of ancient Chinese wares at the time, and himself a benefactor of the Museum, George Eumorfopolos, was willing to underwrite an expedition to China to investigate the finds and share the proceeds with the Museum. As an experienced traveller with connections to the Museum – and no wartime commitments – Torday was an ideal person to look into the matter for the Trustees. But it would be essential, Sir Hercules concluded, that Torday travel as a British subject. The Trustees agreed and the abortive application for naturalisation made on Torday's behalf.

The final blow came as war ended. Again the issue was nationality. The town of Torda, where Torday's estates were located, was ceded to Romania as the boundary with Hungary was redefined. Torday was informed that he could keep his lands on condition that he became a Romanian citizen. He refused, preferring to remain Hungarian. He lost his inheritance. Despite this, he continued to be regarded with suspicion in Hungary itself as a result of his failure to return during the War years – though as a leading member of the Hungarian community in London after the War he was a point of contact for visiting Hungarian intellectuals and published a number of articles about Central Africa in popular journals in Hungary. In the 1920s he was approached to see if he would accept the professorship of anthropology in the newly created department at the University of Pècs. In the end, however, objections from within Hungary itself prevented his taking up the appointment. It would have been his only formal position in the discipline to which he had devoted the main efforts of his adult life.

Torday became involved in work with the Save the Children International Union on problems in Africa, and with the International Institute of African Languages and Cultures of which he was 'one of the leading minds' (Malinowski 1931). However, it was the job of completely redrafting the volume on Africa in the *Descriptive Sociology* series, which he started in the mid-1920s, that was to occupy the remaining years of his life. Vast as the undertaking was, it was again essentially a documentary one, archival in character. It is odd, then, that after his death Malinowski portrayed Torday as a foremost international scholar in the field of anthropology, a respected fellow-traveller. Torday was no diffusionist; but nor had he been particularly drawn to the school of functionalism other than in its proclamation of the virtues of field experience. His area of academic interest remained exclusively that of western Bantu studies. Indeed, the enormous compilation of literature about Africa in the *Descriptive Sociology* volume has more in common with the *Cambridge History of Africa* than the *Ethnographic Survey of Africa*, at least in its citation of sources and its concern for the historical basis of African culture. This, too, was not an especially fashionable perspective. If Maitland's proposition was to merge anthropology into history, Evans-Pritchard, more than a generation later, was to proclaim that anthropology was only *like* history, an interpretative art and not a natural science (1950, 1962). Torday could readily seem old-fashioned in his apparent adherence to the earlier position.

In some of his last writings, however, Torday's views began to take on a more enduring form, just as the quality of the documentary evidence he collected in the field had done. He had, right from his first discussions with Read and Joyce, veered towards an 'anthropological' approach to objects. What this meant was never entirely clear, except perhaps that it involved documenting the function of objects, often more as an act of faith than as part of any integrated study. Thus, whilst welcoming the publication of one of the first surveys of African art, Von Sydow's *Handbuch der afrikanischen Plastik*, Torday regretted that it dealt only in the physical appearance of objects, adopting a purely artistic perspective. 'In many cases', he pointed out, 'technique, execution and shape are trammelled by tradition and vary according to the emotions the finished object is intended to arouse' (1931e, 243). These may not be the same sentiments that the objects arouse out of context. The point is well made, none the less so for having since become a familiar enough starting-point in the discussion of the anthropology of art.

However, Torday went further. The development of the anthropological approach, he believed, was hindered in part by the nature of the vocabulary available to it – in particular the limitations of the terms 'idol' and 'fetish', a word 'which has been such a nuisance to all of us' (1927b, 117). In an important article (1929h) Torday sought to redefine the field as far as certain classes of magical device and ancestral sculpture in the Lower Congo are concerned. The result is a *tour de force* of interpretation. Torday started from an analysis of western Bantu ideas of the nature of spirit and of animating forces. He discussed the historical circumstances in which certain types of figure were introduced; and he showed how Teke figures acquired in time of war become reclassified and reanimated by the Kongo captors of the sculpture, creating a different kind of entity.

In none of this discussion does Torday dwell on the fact that some would have been inclined to replace the term 'fetish' for the objects he was talking about with another word – 'art'. Art and ritual, art and medicine are collapsed together in indigenous categories and should be treated together, not separated out in the terminology itself. His inclination was to replace 'fetish', 'idol' and similar terms with their indigenous equivalent. The important thing was to divest analysis of its prejudicial framework, the better to recover a genuine expression of indigenous meaning. In that he is much closer than were many of his contemporaries to what has come to be the position of modern anthropologists and art historians, the latter

Double wood cup. Wongo.
1910.4–20.11. H. 16.5 cm.

too now recognising the significance of insight based on their own original field research to the discussion of the visual traditions of Africa.

Torday was never in the sway of any greater version of reality and truth that he wished to promote. His interests, as they had always been, were essentially those of someone committed to tinkering with the technicalities of adequately reproducing African forms of expression. However, in the light of a growing sense of the complexity of African culture it was not now a question of establishing the broad sequence of external events which an interest in a certain kind of history implied. Rather it had become a matter of transistorising the intricacies of African thought.

Torday died on 9 May 1931 at the age of fifty-six subsequent to an operation. In 1905 he had recorded in a letter one, entirely fictitious, version of his own biography – that which he imagined Frobenius to be disseminating about him: 'Torday, ay yes, heard about the fellow, sent to London after disgracing his family and got a place there – I think he brushed people's boots in the hall of the British Museum; being chucked out there, he came to the Congo trying to make people believe he was an Ethnographer' (27 October). Torday's death certificate gave his profession simply as 'anthropologist'.

Bibliography

Unpublished sources

A number of relevant archives are held by the British Museum. The primary source of information about the collections themselves are the various Registers which contain documentation and details of provenance concerning the objects in the Torday collection. In addition there are three volumes of papers comprising Torday's original fieldnotes as sent to and annotated by T.A. Joyce, together with Torday's letters to Joyce written between 1905 and 1909. All these are held by the Department of Ethnography (Museum of Mankind). The Department of Medieval and Later Antiquities holds a number of letters from Torday to C.H. Read, whilst the Central Archives contains Reports to Trustees which discuss Torday's association with the British Museum.

Two other institutions hold related material. Torday's correspondence with Henry Balfour is in the Pitt-Rivers Museum, Oxford, and the Diary of the 1907–9 expedition kept by Hilton-Simpson is in the Royal Anthropological Institute, London.

Torday's writings

TORDAY, E., 1905. 'Notes on the Natives of the Kwilu, Congo Free State', *Man*, 5, pp. 135–8
—— 1909. 'Ethnographical Researches in the Kasai District', *The Geographical Journal*, XXXIV, p. 214
—— 1910a. 'Land and Peoples of the Kasai Basin', *The Geographical Journal*, XXXV, pp. 26–57
—— 1910b. 'Le pays et les populations du bassin du Kasai', *Bulletin de la Société d'études coloniales*, XVII, pp. 677–712 (a French translation of 1910a)
—— 1911a. Review of W.J. Edmondston-Scott, *Elements of Negro Religion, Man*, 19, pp. 30–1
—— 1911b. 'A neolithic site in Katanga', *Man*, 26, p. 38
—— 1911c. 'Bushongo Mythology', *Folklore*, XXII, pp. 41–7

—— 1911d. Review of Northcote Thomas, *Anthropological Report on the Edo-Speaking Peoples of Nigeria, Folklore*, XXII, pp. 391–8
—— 1911e. 'Der Tofoke', *Mitteilungen der Anthropologischen Gesellschaft in Wien*, 41, pp. 189–202
—— 1912a. 'Primitive Eugenics', *Mendel Journal*, September, pp. 1–7
—— 1912b. Review of J. Bland-Smith, *Man and Beast in Ethiopia, Man*, 35, p. 64
—— 1913a. *Camp and Tramp in African Wilds*, Seeley, Service and Co., London
—— 1913b. 'The New Congo Collection', *Museum Journal*, IV, pp. 13–32
—— 1913c. 'Note on Unusual Form of Tatu', *Man*, 2, p. 3
—— 1913d. Comment on a paper by Sir H.H. Johnston, 'A survey of the Ethnography of Africa', *Journal of the Royal Anthropological Institute*, XLIII, pp. 415–16
—— 1913e. Review of Rev. A.L. Kitching, *The Backwaters of the Nile* and Cullen Goldsbury and Hubert Sheane, *The Great Plateau of Northern Rhodesia, Folklore*, XXIV, pp. 264–9
—— 1914. 'A Kongo-videk nepeinek eletebol', *Foldr. Kozl*, 42
—— 1915a. Review of R. Gaillard and L. Poutrin, *Etude Anthropologique des populations des Régions du Tchad et du Kanem, Man*, 26, pp. 43–4
—— 1915b. Review of A. de Calonne, *Etudes Bakongo, Man*, 29, pp. 46–7
—— 1917a. 'The Zulu Cult of the Dead', *Man*, 121, p. 178
—— 1917b. Review of Adolphe Louis Curean, *Savage Man in Central Africa, Man*, 23, pp. 34–5
—— 1918. 'Husbandry in the Congo', *Man*, 83, pp. 154–8
—— 1919. 'The Northern Babunda', *Man*, 19, pp. 49–55
—— 1921. 'Culture and Environment; Cultural Differences among the various branches of the Batetela', *Journal of the Royal Anthropological Institute*, LI, pp. 370–84
—— 1922a. Review of John Roscoe, *Twenty-five Years in East Africa, Man*, 18, p. 29
—— 1922b. Review of R.P. Van Wing, S.J., *Etudes Bakongo: Histoire et Sociologie, Man*, 50, pp. 78–80
—— 1924. 'Note on certain figurines of forged iron formerly made by the Bushongo of the Belgian Congo', *Man*, 24, p. 17
—— 1925a. *On the Trail of the Bushongo, an account of a remarkable and hitherto unknown African people, their origin, art, high social and political organization and*

culture, derived from the author's personal experience amongst them, Seeley, Service and Co., London
—— 1925b. *Causeries Congolaises*, Vromant, Brussels
—— 1925c. Review of Cuthbert Christy, *Big Game and Pygmies, Man*, 74, pp. 126–7
—— 1926. 'Art et métiers Bushongo', *Nervie*, 9–10, pp. 12–22 (a French translation of 1925a, ch. XIX)
—— 1927a. 'Sex ratios and cultural contact', *Man*, 24, p. 39
—— 1927b. Review of Capt. R.S. Rattray, *Religion and Art in Ashanti, Man*, 73, pp. 117–18
—— 1927c. Review of P. Amaury Talbot, *The Peoples of Southern Nigeria, Man*, 74, pp. 118–19
—— 1927d. Review of A.W. Cardinall, *In Ashanti and Beyond, Man*, 75, p. 119
—— 1927e. Review of T. Alexander Barnes, *An African Eldorado, Man*, 89, p. 139
—— 1928a. 'The Influence of the Kingdom of Kongo on Central Africa', *Africa*, I, pp. 157–69
—— 1928b. 'Dualism in Western Bantu Religion and Social Organisation', *Journal of the Royal Anthropological Institute*, LVIII, pp. 225–45
—— 1928c. 'Big game from the air', letter to *The Times*, 1 November
—— 1928d. Review of Von Bruno Gutmann, *Das Recht der Dschagga, Man*, 152, p. 212
—— 1929a. 'Bride-price, dower or settlement', *Man*, 3, pp. 5–8
—— 1929b. Obituary of Paul Sarasin, *Man*, 85, p. 113
—— 1929c. 'Bride-price, an answer', *Man*, 107, p. 148
—— 1929d. 'Azande folklore', *Man*, 125, p. 164
—— 1929e. Review of Monroe N. Work, *A Bibliography of the Negro in Africa and America, Man*, 37, p. 178
—— 1929f. 'The morality of African races', *International Journal of Ethics*, 39:2, pp. 167–76
—— 1929g. 'The principles of Bantu marriage', *Africa*, II, pp. 255–90
—— 1929h. 'Le fetichisme, l'idolatrie et la sorcellerie des Bantus occidentaux', *Anthropologie*, IXL, pp. 431–54
—— 1930a. *Descriptive Sociology: African Races*, Williams and Norgate, London
—— 1930b. 'Nzambi Mpungu, the God of the Bakongo', *Man*, 3, p. 3
—— 1930c. Review of Rev. P. Fr. Bosch, *Les Banyamwezi, Peuple de l'Afrique Orientale, Man*, 81, pp. 107–8
—— 1930d. Review of H.R. Herman

Hodge, *Gazetteer of Ilorin Province, Africa,* III, p. 378
—— 1930e. Review of A. Ihle, *Alte Konigreish Kongo, Africa,* III, pp. 378–9
—— 1930f. Review of S.J. Hogben, *Muhammaden Emirates of Nigeria, Africa,* III, pp. 541–3
—— 1931a. 'The child's place in African religion', *Revue Internationale de l'Enfant,* 11 (64), pp. 331–53
—— 1931b. 'The Things that Matter to the West African', *Man,* 31, pp. 110–13
—— 1931c. Review of Door P. Basiel Tanghe, *De ziel van het Ngbandivolk, De Ngbandi naar het leven geschetst* and *De Ngbandi Geschiedkundige Bijtragen, Man,* 53, pp. 52–3
—— 1931d. 'Still-birth and infantile mortality from the social and economic point of view . . . Central Africa', Save the Children International Union
—— 1931e. Review of E. von Sydow, *Handbuch der afrikanischen Plastik Vol. 1, Africa,* IV, pp. 243–5
—— 1931f. Review of Dr Gunther Spannaus, *Züge aus der politischen Organisation Afrikanischer Völker und Staaten, Africa,* IV, pp. 369–70

TORDAY, E., and JOYCE, T. A. 1905. 'Notes on the Ethnography of the Ba-Mbala', *Journal of the Royal Anthropological Institute,* XXXV, pp. 398–426
—— 1906a. 'Notes on the Ethnography of the Ba-Yaka. With Supplementary Note to ''Notes on the Ethnography of the Ba-Mbala''', *Journal of the Royal Anthropological Institute,* XXXVI, pp. 39–59
—— 1906b. 'Notes on the Ethnography of the Ba-Huana', *Journal of the Royal Anthropological Institute,* XXXVI, pp. 272–301
—— 1907a. 'Notes on the Southern Ba-Mbala', *Man,* 7, pp. 81–4
—— 1907b. 'On the Ethnology of the South-Western Congo Free State', *Journal of the Royal Anthropological Institute,* 37, pp. 133–56
—— 1911. *Notes ethnographiques sur les peuples communement appelés Bakuba ainsi que sur les peuplades apparentées : Les Bushongo,* Musée du Congo Belge, Brussels
—— 1922. *Notes ethnographiques sur les peuplades habitant les bassins du Kasai et du Kwango orientale ; peuplades de la forêt ; peuplades des prairies,* Musée du Congo Belge, Brussels

Related writings

ANON. 1909. 'A Scientific Expedition on the Upper Congo', *The Times,* 16 August
—— 1931. 'African Society : Review of Emil Torday, *Descriptive Sociology : African Races, Times Literary Supplement,* 26 February
—— 1931. Obituary, Emil Torday, *The Times,* 11 May
BALFOUR, H., 1910. Comment on E. Torday's 'Land and Peoples of the Kasai', *The Geographical Journal,* XXXV, pp. 55–6
—— 1912. Review of E. Torday and T.A. Joyce, 'Les Bushongo', *Man,* 25, pp. 45–8
HADDON, A.C., 1910. Comment on E. Torday's *Land and Peoples of the Kasai, The Geographical Journal,* XXXV, p. 55
HILTON-SIMPSON, MELVILLE W., 1911. *Land and Peoples of the Kasai,* Constable and Co., London
—— 1932. Obituary, Emil Torday, *Man,* 54, p. 48
JOYCE, T.A., 1909. 'On a Carved Wooden Cup from the Bakuba', *Man,* 9, pp. 1–3
—— 1910a. 'On a Wooden Portrait-Statue from the Bushongo People of the Kasai District, Belgian Congo', *Man,* 10, pp. 1–2
—— 1910b. 'Note on the Pigment-Blocks of the Bushongo People of the Kasai District, Belgian Congo', *Man,* 10, p. 81–2
—— 1913. Comment on a paper by Sir H.H. Johnston, 'A survey of the Ethnography of Africa', *Journal of the Royal Anthropological Institute,* XLIII, pp. 415–19
—— 1925a. 'The Portrait-Statue of Mikope Mbula, 110th Paramount Chief of the Bushongo', *Man,* 25, pp. 185–6
—— 1925b. 'Babunda weaving', *Jahrbuch für prähistorische und etnografische Kunst,* I, pp. 105–10
—— 1932. Obituary, Emil Torday, *Man,* 55, pp. 48–9
JOHNSTON, H.H., 1910. Comment on E. Torday's 'Land and Peoples of the Kasai', *The Geographical Journal,* XXXV, pp. 54–5
KEITH, A., 1911. 'On Certain Physical Characteristics of the Negroes of the Congo Free State and Nigeria, being a Report on material supplied by Mr. E. Torday, Mr. T.A. Joyce, Mr. P.A. Talbot and Mr. Frank Corner, MRCS', *Journal of the Royal Anthropological Institute,* XLI, pp. 40–71
MALINOWSKI, BRONISLAW, 1931. Obituary, Emil Torday, *The Times,* 14 May

MARETT, R.R., 1926. Review of E. Torday, *Causeries Congolaises, Man,* 56, p. 91
NOEL-BUXTON, LORD, 1931. Obituary, Emil Torday, *The Times,* 14 May
1899. *Notes and Queries on Anthropology,* Harrison, London
READ, CHARLES HERCULES, 1905. *Questionnaire ethnographique . . . par C-H. Read, T.A. Joyce, N.W. Thomas et E. Torday,* Instituts Solvay, Brussels
SELIGMAN, BRENDA Z., 1925. Review of E. Torday, *On the Trail of the Bushongo, Man,* pp. 144–5
SMITH, E.W., 1931. Review of E. Torday, *Descriptive Sociology : African Races, Man,* 51, pp. 50–1

Other sources and references

BALFOUR, H., 1893. *The Evolution of Decorative Art : an essay upon its development as illustrated by the art of modern races of Mankind,* Rivington Percival, London
BASSANI, EZIO, and McLEOD, MALCOLM, n.d. *Jacob Epstein Collector,* Associazone Poro, Milan
BIEBUYCK, DANIEL, 1985. *The Arts of Zaire, Volume 1 : Southwestern Zaire,* University of California Press, Berkeley and Los Angeles
BOURGEOIS, ARTHUR P., 1980. 'Kakungu among Yaka and Suku', *African Arts,* XIV, 1, pp. 42–6
—— 1988. 'The Jerome L. Joss Mbala drummer', *Arts de l'Afrique Noire,* 65, pp. 12–25 ; 66, pp. 19–29
BRAUNHOLTZ, H.J., 1970. 'Ethnography since Sloane', in the late H.J. Braunholtz (ed. William Fagg), *Sir Hans Sloane and Ethnography,* British Museum, London
CARMICHAEL, ELIZABETH, 1973. *The British and the Maya,* British Museum, London
CLIFFORD, JAMES, 1983. 'Power and Dialogue in Ethnography : Marcel Griaule's Initiation', in George W. Stocking (ed.), *Observers Observed, Essays in Ethnographic Fieldwork,* History of Anthropology, 1, University of Wisconsin Press, pp. 121–56
CONRAD, JOSEPH, 1902. *Heart of Darkness,* J.M. Dent and Sons, London
CORNET, JOSEPH, 1982. *Art Royal Kuba,* Edizioni Sipiel, Milan
DALTON, O.M., 1898. *Report on Ethnographic Museums in Germany,* Her Majesty's Stationery Office, London
DERAIN, ANDRÉ, 1955. *Lettres à Vlaminck,* Flammarion, Paris

EVANS-PRITCHARD, E.E., 1937. *Witchcraft, Oracles and Magic among the Azande*, Clarendon Press, Oxford

—— 1950. 'Social Anthropology: Past and Present', *Man*, L, pp. 118–24

—— 1962. 'Anthropology and History', in E.E. Evans-Pritchard, *Essays in Social Anthropology*, Faber and Faber, London

ELLIOT-SMITH, G., 1924. *Elephants and Ethnologists*, Kegan Paul, London

FAGG, WILLIAM, 1965. *Tribes and Forms in African Art*, Methuen, London

FELIX, MARC, 1987. *100 Peoples of Zaire and their Sculpture*, Zaire Basin Art History Research Foundation, Brussels

FORBATH, PETER, 1977. *The River Congo*, Harper and Row, London

FRAZER, J.G., 1890. *The Golden Bough, A Study in Comparative Religion*, MacMillan & Co., London

FROBENIUS, LEO, 1907. *Im Schatten des Kongostaates*, Georg Reimer, Berlin

FRY, ROGER, 1920. *Vision and Design*, Chatto and Windus, London

GRIAULE, M., 1948. *Dieu d'Eau: Entretiens avec Ogotommêli*, Paris

HADDON, A.C., 1895. *Evolution in Art as illustrated by the Life-histories of Designs*, W. Scott Ltd, London

—— 1903. 'Anthropology, its position and needs', *Journal of the Anthropological Institute*, XXXIII, pp. 11–23

HOCART, A.M., 1954. *Social Origins*, Watts, London

JOHNSTON, H.H., 1908. *George Grenfell and the Congo*, 2 vols, Hutchinson, London

JOYCE, T.A., 1912. *South American Archaeology*, Macmillan and Co. and Phillip Lee Warner, London

—— 1914. *Mexican Archaeology*, Phillip Lee Warner, London

—— 1916. *Central American and West Indian Archaeology*, Phillip Lee Warner, London

JOYCE, T.A., and DALTON, O.M., 1910. *Handbook of the Ethnographical Collections*, British Museum, London

LANGHAM, IAN, 1981. *The Building of British Social Anthropology: W.H.R. Rivers and his Cambridge disciples in the development of kinship studies, 1898–1931*, Dordrecht, London

MACK, JOHN, 1975. 'W.H.R. Rivers: The Contexts of Social Anthropology', D.Phil thesis, University of Oxford

—— 1989. 'Documenting the Cultures of Southern Zaire: the photographs of the Torday expeditions, 1900–1909', Paper read at the Triennal meetings of the Arts Council of the African Studies

Association of America, Washington D.C., June

—— forthcoming. Working title: *Catalogue of the Emil Torday Collection*, British Museum Publications, London

MAESEN, A., 1967. *Art of the Congo*, Walker Art Gallery, Minneapolis

MAITLAND, F.W., 1911. *Collected Papers*, 3 vols, Cambridge University Press

MEURANT, GEORGES, 1986. *Shoowa Design, African Textiles from the Kingdom of the Kuba*, Thames and Hudson, London

MOORE, DAVID, 1984. *The Torres Straits Collections of A.C. Haddon, a Descriptive Catalogue*, British Museum Publications

1980. *Observers of Man* (prepared by R. and A. Poignant and P. Wallis), Royal Anthropological Institute

PENNIMAN, T.K., 1935. *A Hundred Years of Anthropology*, Duckworth, London

PICTON, J., 1986. 'The Art Historian as Ventriloquist, or do Images Really Talk?', paper presented at the 29th Annual Meeting of the African Studies Association of America, Madison

PLANQUERT, MICHEL, 1930. *Les Sociétés secrètes chez les Bayaka*, J. Kuyl-Otto, Louvain

QUIGGIN, A. HINGSTON, 1942. *Haddon the Headhunter*, Cambridge University Press

READ, CHARLES HERCULES, 1891. 'On the origin and sacred character of certain ornaments of the S.E. Pacific', *Journal of the Anthropological Institute*, XXI, pp. 45–57

—— 1906. 'Anthropology at the Universities', *Man*, 38, pp. 56–9

READ, C.H., and DALTON, O.M., 1899. *Antiquities from the City of Benin and other parts of West Africa in the British Museum*, British Museum, London

RIVERS, W.H.R., 1900. 'A genealogical method of collecting social and vital statistics', *Journal of the Royal Anthropological Institute*, XXX, 74–82

—— 1906. *The Todas*, MacMillan and Co., London

—— 1913. 'Report on anthropological research outside America', *Carnegie Institute of Washington Publications*, 200, pp. 5–28

—— 1914. *The History of Melanesian Society*, 2 vols, Cambridge University Press

ROSENWALD, JEAN, B., 1974. 'Kuba King Figures', *African Arts*, VII, 26–31

SELIGMAN, C.G. and B.Z., 1932. *Pagan Tribes of the Nilotic Sudan*, Routledge and Sons, London

SLOBODIN, RICHARD, 1978. *W.H.R. Rivers*, Columbia University Press, New York

SPENCER, W.B., and GILLEN, F.J., 1890. *The Native Tribes of Central Australia*, MacMillan and Co., London

STENGERS, JEAN, and VANSINA, JAN, 1985. 'King Leopold's Congo, 1868–1908', in Roland Oliver and G.N. Sanderson (eds), *Cambridge History of Africa*, vol. 6 (1870–1907), Cambridge University Press

STOCKING, GEORGE W., Jr. (ed.), 1983. *Observers Observed, Essays in Ethnographic Fieldwork*, History of Anthropology, 1, University of Wisconsin Press

—— 1984. *Functionalism Historicized. Essays on British Social Anthropology*, History of Anthropology, 2, University of Wisconsin Press

—— 1985. *Objects and Others. Essays on Museums and Material Culture*, History of Anthropology, 3, University of Wisconsin Press

TYLOR, E.B., 1871. *Primitive Culture*, 2 vols, John Murray, London

URRY, JAMES, 1972. 'Notes and Queries on Anthropology and the development of field methods in British Anthropology, 1870–1920', *Proceedings of the Royal Anthropological Institute*, 45–57

—— 1982. 'From Zoology to Ethnology', *Canberra Anthropology*, 5, 58–85

—— 1984. 'A history of field methods', in R.F.G. Ellen (ed.), *Ethnographic Research, A guide to general conduct*, Academic Press, London

VANSINA, JAN, 1972. 'Ndop: Royal Statues among the Kuba', in Douglas Fraser and Herbert M. Cole (eds), *African Art and Leadership*, University of Wisconsin Press, Madison

—— 1978. *The Children of Woot, A History of the Kuba Peoples*, University of Wisconsin Press, Madison

WERNER, ALICE, 1906. *The Native Races of British Central Africa*, Archibald Constable, London

—— 1910. 'The Bushongo', *Journal of the African Society*, IX, pp. 206–12

Index

References in italic type are to black and white illustrations; references in bold type are to colour plates.